Island
Boy

Island
Boy

J. Michael Woods

gatekeeper press™
Columbus, Ohio

ISLAND BOY

Published by Gatekeeper Press
2167 Stringtown Rd, Suite 109
Columbus, OH 43123-2989
www.GatekeeperPress.com

The editorial work for this book is entirely the product of the author. Gatekeeper Press did not participate in and is not responsible for any aspect of this elements.

Library of Congress Control Number: 2022930963

ISBN (paperback): 9781662925191
eISBN: 9781662925207

TABLE OF CONTENTS

ENDORSEMENTS

This amazing man, John Woods, is a prime example of an overcomer! God had a plan for John's life and has used him to be a blessing to others. John served our Church as Interim Pastor, Religious Education Director, Bible Teacher, and Youth Leader. He and his wife Janet are a blessing to all who know them. John has an inspiring story and my wife, Ann, and I are looking forward to reading *Island Boy*.

Pastor Ken Pennell
Former Missionary to Ecuador
Retired Pastor of Fort Pierce Alliance Church

* * *

I first met John about twenty years ago when he became a GED teacher with the school system. I had been teaching GED and was moving on to be our youth coordinator for the same school system. My office was located down the block for some time, (maybe 6 months) then my office was moved back to the school where we would become coworkers. I inquired about several students I had taught, and John informed me that they had indeed passed their GED. Now this is no small feat, and I certainly was surprised at their accomplishments. I knew that John had something special to offer these students, and many more, who needed a second and third chance.

I have come to respect John's strong faith in Jesus Christ. That is what he always placed first in his life, along with his family and friends. I have watched John thrive in his faith for over twenty years now. John could always lift me up when he didn't even know he was doing so. He used to joke with me that I always looked at the bright side, and could find positive momentary humor, but just like *cream*, it was his strong faith that always came to the top in any situation.

Over the years, throughout our careers, John and I have shared many stories. Once I told John about winning a trip though the company I had worked for in 1975. I lived in Fairfax, VA at the time and had won an all-expense paid trip from Washington DC to Miami Fl. I was telling John about this, and he proceeded to inform me that the owner of the company had flown his wife, Janet to various places in the U.S. At that point, I was amazed we actually both knew this person.

Numerous times John would have knowledge and involvement in the very thing being discussed. I have always encouraged John to write a book about his unique experiences, and I am glad that he is doing so. I believe it can inspire others and help them find and keep faith in Christ. God Bless!

Gary Hansard, Retired, BA. EDS.
Presently serving as Claiborne County Veterans Service Officer

* * *

What a special honor to write an endorsement for my husband. I have witnessed the unfolding of this memoir. The life this dear man has lived is now on paper for all to read. Recording the actual events of his extraordinary life is only the beginning. Throughout countless hours of John's writing, I saw him stop, pray, and make certain he explained the spiritual significance of what he had gone through. Living a purposeful life means learning from past experiences. John has utilized these lessons to equip himself with compassion and understanding for others. I, and so many others, are recipients of John's goodness and kindness. As you read *Island Boy*, you will get a glimpse of this servant of God I am privileged to walk beside.

Janet Woods Teacher
Author of Deskmate to Helpmeet

* * *

My name is Gail Leonard. I am the Headmaster of Heritage Christian Academy in East Tennessee. I have known John Woods for many, many years, both on a professional and a personal level. When I think of John Woods, three words come to mind – honesty, integrity, and long suffering. John is a true example of a modern-day Job of the Old Testament. John, like Job, is a true man of God in every sense of the word. He has suffered countless hardships, persevered, and overcome great obstacles. Where many would have given up in such circumstances, John waited with unwavering faith and patience for God to move. John's relationship with God is a living testament to the miracles that still happen today to those who wait upon the Lord.

Gail Leonard
Headmaster Heritage Christian Academy
New Tazewell, Tennessee

* * *

John Woods' life and testimony is a mosaic of God's amazing grace. His story is a fascinating read of how God worked to bring those pieces together, give new life by faith in Christ, and raise up a faithful servant of Christ and his church. I can't wait to see the whole book. John's life continues to be lived as a witness of the gospel's power today. It is a tremendous honor to serve as his pastor, and you'll be tremendously blessed by his testimony. Come and hear as he tells you what God has done for his soul (Ps. 66:16).

Wayne Meadows, DMin
Poplar Springs Baptist Church
Hiram, Georgia

PREFACE

Why Write This Book

The Apostle Paul calls us Ambassadors for Christ. An ambassador is an authorized messenger or representative. As a Christian, representing Christ means to go and tell about His love, power, and goodness. *Island Boy* captures the grandeur of God on display in a life facing incredible odds.

In *Island Boy*, J. Michael Woods attempts to say, "Thank You!" to this God who came to him and poured out His love, so that he could have life more abundantly. Isaiah 2:5 says, "Let us walk in the light of the Lord." As we do so, let us represent Him by telling of His goodness. He is *The Light of the World!*

THROUGH MY EYES

J. Michael Woods is my brother, but I call him Johnny. As a young girl, I knew that my brother was different from others, as he suffered with epilepsy. Our strong bond began early because of his epilepsy and the death of my father when I was only five. We took on the role of protector for each other. I have fond memories of riding in the back seat of our grandparents' car as I sucked my two middle fingers. Sometimes at bedtime, I found myself rubbing his silk shirt between my fingers and him twirling my hair until I fell asleep.

As early as six years old, my brother being eight, I knew that he had a great love and a deeper understanding of God than I did . Around that time, our country was being threatened with war from Russian missiles located in Cuba. Being from Florida, we would have to prepare and hide under our desks. I remember crying, telling my brother that I didn't want to die, and what if I didn't get to go to Heaven. He said, "Please don't cry, I promise, you will go to Heaven with me because God sees your heart and you are an innocent child" How did he know that at eight?

Throughout the years, there were times that were not easy for him; not only was he dealing with his epilepsy, but he was not able to attend school as I was. He was left out of a lot of things others got to do. That used to hurt me and I would see him cry and not understand why, but he always found a way to make it through.

When the time came for him to step out on his own and go to college, you may ask, "How, without being able to go to school?" It was common knowledge in our family that his doctors' reports said with such severe seizures, writing and learning could be a challenge. I say, ...BUT GOD!!

I have seen with my own eyes how God has been with him every step of the way and has guided him through life, marriage, and raising a beautiful son. He has always put God first in his life, and it shows in his home and his giving of himself to others.

He is the first person I call to pray for me, family or friends because I know that he will. He is my guiding compass and I thank God every day that he made Johnny my brother.

I sometimes stand in awe at all John has accomplished, and then I say ... BUT GOD!!

Love you much, Johnny Cakes,
Your sister, Marie

P.S. When you turn the pages of Island Boy, you will see God's Glory on display.

Chapter One

STRUGGLES, FAITH, AND CHOICES

¹⁷Though the fig tree should not blossom,
**   nor fruit be on the vines,**
the produce of the olive fail
**   and the fields yield no food,**
the flock be cut off from the fold
**   and there be no herd in the stalls,**
¹⁸ yet I will rejoice in the Lord;
**   I will take joy in the God of my salvation.**
Habakkuk 3:17-18

The name Habakkuk means *Embracer*. We all need to hold to something much bigger than ourselves as we face life's rigorous demands and cruel twists of fate living can bring. The Old Testament prophet inquired why God was quiet and watching while the people of the Southern Kingdom of Judah were being ravaged by a more disobedient people than they. The Chaldeans (Babylonians) had brought their ferocious, wicked actions and captivity upon the Southern Kingdom.

I, too, wondered why God seemed to be quiet, not caring about my years as a teenager. Life became upside down not long before I was turning thirteen years of age, ravaged by epileptic seizures, isolation, loneliness, and yes, sometimes unbelief. The questions would pour from my soul, "Why God...? Can't you hear me? Have you abandoned me?" Unlike the people of Judah, I had not built altars and made pacts with idolaters. I had been taught by my grandmother to pray as a small three-year-old boy. She knelt beside my bed with me and would say as I repeated, "Now I lay me down to sleep, I pray the Lord my soul to keep, and if I die before I wake, I pray, O' God, my soul you'll take. Amen." I then would ask God to bless my family. Some today would ask, "Why mention dying in a child's nighttime prayer?" One must say, in today's world, it would not be deemed acceptable. Back in the day, people had often gone through so much that they acknowledged dying as a part of living. Perhaps we are weak in not wanting to train our children to have a healthy respect for the part of life that is hard to accept, and to trust God for the comfort they will need.

I developed a strong *childlike faith, one anchored* in the God whom I believed loved me so very much. This trust would be threatened by strong headwinds that would grow even stronger, as days and the foreseeable years ahead were to promise heavy and more powerful storms. These winds of life were to become gales of hurricane force, fluctuating in intensity. Yes, the threatening Satan likes to destroy developing faith early, yet will try at any stage of faith, and is cunning in doing so. He attempts to destroy the trust one has in an all-loving God through any gateway we may allow him to enter. Satan used deceit to cause the fall of humankind. We can hear Eve's thoughts as she begins to doubt that God clearly commanded, she and Adam should not eat of that one tree. Prompted by Satan, her thoughts were, *certainly God does not mean we cannot eat of a tree so beautiful, having such luscious fruit.* Eve ate from it; Adam agreed with her and ate of it also. Adam rationalized, beauty and knowledge God would not keep from them. Today, an example of this would be, "But we love each other, so why can't we sleep together? God surely could not mean to keep this beautiful experience from us." In reality, God forbids this before marriage; to spare us from hurt later. He calls it fornication, which is sin, not love.

Here are a few deceiving gateways. Don't let Satan in!

- *God is keeping enjoyment from me.*

- *God doesn't care.*

- *If God loves me, then why is he allowing this?*

- *You just think there is a God.*

- *I've got this, I don't need to read Scripture, pray, or attend church.*

> **Yet you do not know what tomorrow will bring. What is your life? For you are a mist that appears for a little time and then vanishes.**
> James 4:14

Satan's number one tool is SIN, and he weaponizes it through deceit and lies. If allowed, he will destroy one's ability to trust. Satan is the ultimate mind game player. It is often during hard times that he sows his seed of mistrust. In good times, he tries to take your focus off the importance of placing your faith in God, and coaxes you to trust in self, and the things of this world. He tries to usurp God's Holiness and Glory with *Garden of Eden mentality.* Satan pushes the falsehood that God is keeping something from us.

I had much time to think, being alone. God seemingly was not answering. His silence caused me to ask how I had gotten into the condition I found myself. My childlike faith had come to a **T** in the road. My imagination saw a road called faith, not well traveled. The road in the other direction had no name, but to travel on it, childlike faith had to be left behind and replaced with what would be found as you traveled it. The road looked welcoming, and I could see in my mind's eye that it was well used. Surely God would want to bear my hardship of loneliness by giving me a gentle road to travel and lead me back to society where I could go to school and have my friends. "But what about trust?" I asked myself. We need to operate in what we know, and what I knew was to trust God; not to do so would be folly. Trusting in God had been my mainstay as a young child. In the book of Hebrews, I had read and reread about the heroes of faith. I had begun reading the Bible, in which these stories are found, at about eight years of age. It was their faith in a Creator God that had brought them through so much. They each were faced with daunting hardships, but what they had in common was their faith in God.

You may be asking, "Who is he that isolation and loneliness could be so overwhelming? Why would he be pondering so deep in his soul and asking where God was, and if God really heard and cared about this one solitary life?" Well, this boy would become Island Boy.

I was living on what is known as a spoil island. It had been made from the deepening of the channel of the Indian River Lagoon. Part of the Intracoastal Waterway, it is used and traveled on by barges, yachts, and boats of all sizes. This spoil island was located directly in front of two large sand dikes. They were made by the need to create a deep waterway spurring off from the main lagoon channel toward the mainland. The channel would be used for vessels in need of deeper water to operate, and to dock for loading and unloading.

The port was first used to ship white sand to the Bahamas by barge in the 1960s. Barges would then return with a type of aragonite, used to replace calcium in produce growing soil. Some years later, about 1970 or '71, a new industry would replace the original use. Chrysler Outboard, which had a business in the same location, testing their outboard motors and boats would also eventually be replaced. This new industry would become Harbor Branch Oceanographic Institute. HBOI was founded by J. Seward Johnson, entrepreneur billionaire in collaboration with Edwin Albert Link.[1] Link had become famous in aeronautics. He was notable for inventing the Link Trainer. It was the first flight simulator which helped pilots learn to fly as well as simulate battle techniques for those in the Air Force during the war. Also notable, is the Link, Man In Sea Program, which advanced ocean exploration.[2]

Island boy remained mostly isolated, but from a short distance could observe life down, up, and around the waterway. There were the yachts that would blow at Naked Charlie as he stood on his dock, a tiny island away, plucking feathers from his homegrown chickens for meals that week. Area fishermen named him Nature Boy because he chose only to wear clothes if he went into town. Uncle Bill called him the Old Goat because his long grey goatee resembled one.

One of the largest and most elegant of the yachts I observed was owned by Frances Langford, who had been a famous singer and movie star. She, at the time, was married to Ralph Evinrude, of the renowned Evinrude Outboard Motor Corporation. Also, the tugboats and barges coming and going were quite interesting to watch. Not to be left out, there were three men my grandfather knew who came up to another island on the other side of Naked Charlie's abode. They came up on weekends to fish and drink. Many a Friday and Saturday, late at night, you could hear them singing loudly, "Aye Yi Yippee Ki Yay! Three Men Floating in A Boat. Aye Yi Yippee Ki Yay!" They would repeat this refrain louder as they gulped their beer throughout the night. Most likely they were celebrating their time away from their wives and their "honey-do" lists on the great fishing area known by the locals as Blue Hole and Garfield. Yes, I could see and hear a lot of living going on before me, but my world was like a bubble with little traffic in or out. My young faith was being stretched. Would it fail? This possibility was consequential since my faith was in its infancy stage of trust. I reasoned that stretching sometimes means growth. My doubt would shout, **"I have already been through so much."**

The faithless road enticed me. In my thinking, I heard, *"Come over here, it's easier."* Yet a still small voice in my heart encouraged me to remember the Heroes of Faith. With God's help, I would choose the road less traveled which permitted faith to travel with me. The other roads seemed smoother and wider, but my developing faith was not allowed. No, I would not travel a destination route that would only promise to ease my situation if I followed it. I could not stop trust-

> **...but the righteous shall live by his faith.**
> Habakkuk 2:4b

ing in the God to whom I had learned to pray. After all, I remembered reading in scripture what happened for the Heroes of Faith. Their faith made them strong, and the God of their faith brought good for them out of bad, even if they did not know how it was to be done. If only I would trust and obey the One who had created me, I thought.

Life had dealt some harsh blows, but God... And Cootie had told me...

Oh, Cootie is what I called my loving grandmother. You remember the one who taught me how to pray and trust in someone much bigger than myself. Cootie had told me about how I was left with her and my grandfather by my mother when I was only three months old.

Cootie, Always Supporting Me!
Old Dixie Highway and Taylor Creek Bridge
circa 1953

She told me that I had a sweet mother, but that she had left home at the age of fourteen. She was later found with Jack Woods and was pregnant with my older brother Billy. This saddened Cootie, but she said that she thought it would be best to allow her daughter to marry Jack since he would be the father of her son who was soon to be born. In those days, especially in the South, it was not uncommon for people to marry young. Mary Nell thought she loved him, but Cootie believed the marriage would be short lived.

Let's circle back to how Cootie got her nickname. My older cousin Steve informed me that he heard our grandfather call her this quite frequently. As a small child, being the first of the grandchildren, he just supposed that this was her name. She liked it and told her daughter Althea that it was cute the way Steve said it. She said it sounded better than grandma or grandmother. So, *Cootie* she became, to all the grandchildren that would be born following him. Besides liking her nickname, she enjoyed growing flowers, and roses were her favorite. She called them *rosies*. Cootie and her first born daughter shared the first name Althea. When Althea was born, she was as pretty as a new flower, so Cootie lovingly called her Rosebud.

Jack was gone a lot because he worked transporting barges and was in and out of ports, so much so that he looked at being home as just another port. Billy was born in September of 1949. Mary was fifteen years old. Jack began drinking alcohol, mostly beer. He also had a need to impress others and would buy drinks for all his friends.

Spending money unwisely led to hard times for them. Mary knew if Billy's needs were to be met, and if the light bills were to be paid on time, she would need to find a job to supplement any money Jack would have left over.

As soon as Billy was old enough, Mary found a part time job at a privately owned grocery store as a cashier. They were living in Volusia County Florida, with Daytona being the largest of all the community towns. When Billy was a toddler, Mary was approached by the landlord who had grown weary of ceaseless excuses for the late rent. She promised him that Jack would be back from his job and pay last month's rent and the payment due presently. He demanded, "When?" She replied, "In about two days." The boat Jack worked on did make it back, but in three days. Before coming home, he had spent a large portion of his pay drinking, carousing, and playing Mr. Big Cheese. They had an argument about the rent money and Jack went and volunteered to go out ahead of time on the next vessel. The owner of the apartment returned and set all their meager belongings outside and padlocked the doors. Mary had left to check with her friend to arrange for her to watch Billy that day after three o'clock. She was scheduled to work, but now what? It was almost ready to storm and there lay everything she owned outdoors. Cootie said, "Mary Nell covered everything she could with a few plastic tablecloths that she dug out of the pile of her things setting outside the locked doors." She quickly took Billy to her friend so she would not be late for her shift. The friend asked what was wrong, seeing the fright in Mary's face. While she tried to hold back tears, she replied, "I can't talk right now, I will tell you when I get off work and pick up Billy."

Cootie said, "Honey, we'll talk more, but it is getting late, and I need to fix supper for your Uncle Bill." This name was what most of the grandchildren, including me, called him, except Steve, the eldest grandchild, who often affectionately called him George. Cootie had little interest in being called Grandma, and it is understandable why Uncle Bill resisted being called Grandpa, being much younger.

Totally lost in thought, I took a short walk before supper. I didn't even hear Uncle Bill come up in the boat. I was trying to make sense of it all. I could not help but see the similarity between myself and John the Revelator. He had been exiled to the Isle of Patmos where he was to record the Revelation of Jesus Christ. In the Book of Revelation, he uses imagery to represent the story he is called to tell. This John, sun-burnt, with sand between his toes, tried to embrace the isolation, trusting he too had purpose and a story to tell. The island, on which I now was exiled, found me often confused and desperate for friends and meaning, leaving me with many moments of wanting to end all; But GOD... *He holds us together and protects us from ourselves.*

> **Even before a word is on my tongue, behold, O Lord, you know it altogether. You hem me in, behind and before, and lay your hand upon me. Such knowledge is too wonderful for me; it is high. I cannot attain it.**
> Psalm 139:4-6

I would watch the large boats moving north and south through the channel. It had been dredged to create a deeper waterway, allowing smooth passage. I remembered how God, in Old Testament scripture, would clean out entire cities for their wrongdoing, to establish right. As the prophet asked why, I ended my day in prayer, asking why. God seemed to whisper, "Just as the channel has to be dredged and cleaned out to make it deeper, so too, am I working to increase your depth."

Chapter One Endnotes

1. *https://en.wikipedia.org/wiki/Harbor_Branch_Oceanographic_Institute*
2. *https://en.wikipedia.org/wiki/Link_Trainer*

Chapter Two

LIFE CHANGING EVENTS

Looking from the west cove of the island, down the middle of the two sand dikes, I could picture us coming that first day. There we were, Uncle Bill and I speeding toward this island that I had never seen. It had been years since I had last ridden in a boat. Getting to experience this adventure was exciting. It was during my fifth-grade year, my teacher was Mrs. McLaughlin. She was so kind and devoted to her students. *This year had started with great expectations*! A great teacher, good friends, a God who loves me, and now out on the river, going to a place where I had never gone before. I had high hopes that this day would be adventurous.

However, my twelfth year on earth would bring big changes. Standing upon the island, remembering that first day Uncle Bill and me racing toward it, I could not have imagined the hardships that would attempt to derail me.

Poisoned

Life already had been replete with challenges which had started even before birth. I had been born underweight and placed on special watch, in what today is called neonatal intensive care unit. (NICU) I was later poisoned twice when visiting my mother and older brother Billy. As he tells the story, he did not know why he did these things. He remembers on the first poisoning that he knew where the poison was kept. Its purpose was for killing ground moles, which could destroy one's lawn. They looked like peanuts and were kept in a cabinet just off the kitchen. He climbed up to the top shelf and brought them down. "Johnny," he said, "Do you want some? These are yummy peanuts!" When he said that, I took and ate some, as any toddler would do. Our mother walked in and saw me eating the poison. She frantically picked me up and started shoving her fingers in my mouth to remove them and to keep me from swallowing more. She told Billy to get into the car and she rushed me to the hospital, where she knew Dr. Sinnett would be. He was a friend of my grandparents. He pumped out my stomach. He observed me for a few hours and said, "Well, let's hope we got it all."

A similar incident would happen a few months later when I was three years of age. I was again visiting my mother on Hartman Road in Fort Pierce FL. The town was small in the 1950s, and everyone knew just about everyone else, or was connected in some way. I was with Billy, who was four years older than me, making him seven. He said we had been playing in the front yard, when he noticed the garage door being up. He thought to himself, I wonder what we could find in there. He picked up a small can of varnish and opened it. Knowing how I enjoyed things to drink, as I still do today, He said, "Johnny, drink some of this, it is tasty and good!" Now, what would a 7-year-old know about varnish? Well, he knew enough not to drink it himself. He handed it to me and said, "Yummy! Drink some, Johnny." I took it and gulped it down, and immediately began choking. I started to have trouble breathing, which scared him, and he ran to get our mother. Upon seeing me, she frantically asked, "Billy what have you done?" He showed her the varnish can. Here she was again, just months after the first incident, rushing me back to the hospital to Dr. Sinnett. I was told that he again pumped my stomach but was worried about the possible long-term effects. Reportedly, he told my mother that this was twice in one year, and that if it happened again, he would contact the proper authorities. He gave my grandparents a call and it was decided not to let me go back for a visit by myself until I was older.

As I started the 1st grade, Dr. Sinnett's fear of long-term effects was beginning to manifest itself. Varnish has lead in it, and as we know today, it can cause brain injury. I began to have slight seizures where I would get a dizzy feeling and see the flashing of light in front of my eyes, originating from abnormal brain cell activity. I was withdrawn from school and doctors ordered a spinal tap where fluid could be tested. They wanted to check the cerebral spinal fluid to rule out infection such as meningitis or encephalitis as the cause for my epileptic seizures. This was all done in the hospital.

The Genesis of My Compassion

I must relate here a memory I have of an incident on the last day I attended school that year. A student had asked if he could be excused to use the bathroom. He was denied his request. Awhile later, there was a stench that permeated the air. My classmate had diarrhea running down his leg. The teacher got upset with the student and set him and his desk outside the door in the sunshine. I remembered leaving that day and having to go around him sitting there. The sight of him there in his soiled pants with big flies on him, buzzing all around, hurt my young heart. I can still remember it as if it were yesterday. This was the same teacher who demanded that I write using my right hand, even though I was left hand dominant. Many educators at this time had believed because we live in a right-hand dominant society, that they should insist a student writing with the left hand be made to write right-handed. I suppose they thought that they could change the pattern of the brain. This was later proven to be fallacy. It was done for the right reasons but was wrong, as studies would later show.

There is no exercise better for the heart than reaching down and lifting people up.
John Holmes

These two events helped shape my thinking and compassion in years to come. Yes, one can be right, yet wrong at the same time. It was right that the teacher did not want this student to be playing in the bath-

> **Compassion is passion with a heart.**
> Anonymous

room, but it was wrong for her not to listen to his pleas to use the bathroom. It was also wrong for her to get upset with him and to handle the situation as she did. Minus compassion, right is usually wrong. He missed much more time and was hurt more by ignoring his frantic requests. If only she had let him go with a trusted student if she had doubts.

> Luke 6:31   Matthew 7:12
> **And as you wish others would do to you, do so to them.**
> THE GOLDEN RULE

Without compassion for others, we do not prize humanity created in God's image. I also was touched in that I, myself, had such a sad feeling for him when passing by his desk going home that day. I would later become an advocate for those in unfortunate situations. This was my first re-membrance of feeling sorry for someone and wanting to help change things for them.

Six-Year-Old Johnny

Chapter Three

LOCKED OUT! WHERE DID MARY NELL GO?

As you now know, Mary Nell is my mother; but where is my father? I had met Jack Woods once with Billy when I was nine years old. I already knew that I didn't look like Billy, nor did I even have a similar personality. I could see that my brother and Jack had similar traits of identity. I carried his last name, but something, I felt, was missing. He paid a great deal of attention to Billy, but hardly spoke to me. I was never to see him again, whereas Billy saw him from time to time.

Mom had remarried in 1954, leaving Jack in 1953. As I remember him, Bob was a kind, working man. He was somewhat older than my mother and loved her dearly. What a change from her first husband. Their marriage was to produce my next two siblings, Rose Marie and Robert. He was named Robert Graham Reid after his father with the same name. Unfortunately, their father would die of lung cancer in 1961. He fought a strong and courageous fight. Minutes before he died, he was to regain eyesight and strength and read a beautiful prayer that only he could see on the wall. My grandmother said no one in the room had ever heard it before. Moments later, his spirit left his body.

On the island, Cootie, and I, usually just the two of us, would have many conversations about my feelings concerning who my father was, my seizures, and my hopes for the future. On one occasion, we were putting flowers in the ground, talking about the pretty plants. She would talk right to the flower saying, "They always grow better if you talk to them." She was right, but I knew there had to be an explanation. My query into the why, led me to read about plant life. "Bingo!" One day I said as I read. Plants flourish from carbon dioxide. I told her what we breathe out is carbon dioxide, which is then used by the plant to thrive. I excitedly told her, "God was the first recycler. He doesn't let anything go to waste! not even our spent breath."

We were again planting roses one day and I looked her way. "That story you were telling me in the kitchen last fall, you know, the one about my mother being locked out of her apartment. She was troubled as she left Billy at her friend's house on her way to work." "Well honey, I don't know how far I should go with this." Cootie hesitated.

"Cootie," I said. "You know I have deep suspicions that Jack is not my father. I do not look or act like him, but Billy does.

Besides, you have told me in other conversations that he was silly and had a need to impress others. Won't you tell me what happened to my mother when she had no place for Billy or her to live?"

"Okay, Johnny," she said. "Your mother was in a panic and scared. She was only 18 years old at this time and I surely had regretted allowing her to marry at such a young age. She told me she would not stay home and that I couldn't stop her from loving Jack." I asked Cootie what had happened.

Cootie continued and told me that she made it to work. The customers were saying, "Mary, you're sure not your sweet self today." She had told me that during her break she went into the backroom and cried. The butcher at the store, a man named Peacock, saw her crying. He went in to see about her and asked her what was wrong. She told him about being locked out of her home and did not know where she and Billy would sleep that night or anytime soon. She told Mr. Peacock she could not believe that Jack would spend most of the rent money before coming home after docking. They had an argument about it, and Jack told her to figure it out.

I said to Cootie, "You see! I just knew it! I am not a Woods. I would never do a thing like that. I bet he was chicken to face their landlord. He probably thought my mother would cry to him and that he would feel sorry for her and let her, and Billy stay." I repeated, "I am not a Woods!"

"Well, Honey, that is what is on your birth certificate."

Apparently, Mr. Peacock did have a heart. He explained that his wife's parents lived in Germany and that he met his wife while serving in the U.S. Army in that country. She would often go back to see them and had just left on a ship with their daughter. Cootie thought there may be two daughters, both blonde and blue-eyed. Cootie went on to say that he said to your mother not to worry, but that he owned a big two-story house, and that she and her son could have one of the rooms for a while. Cootie relayed to me that my mother asked him how much he would charge for allowing her to stay there for the time being. He reportedly told her that if she would just clean the house while his wife was in Germany, that it would be enough. Mary took him up on the offer. Jack was back at sea, and Billy and mom now had security and a place to live. Cootie said that travel was slow in those days and that my mother had told her that his wife would be gone for an extended amount of time. I was relieved to know that she and Billy had a place to go and be safe. After a few weeks, my mother reportedly told Cootie that Mr. Peacock was a clean and orderly man, so clean, that when Mary Nell knew that her sister was coming through the Daytona area, she asked her to stop in and see her. Althea was happy to see the nice place she was living, and yes, she saw just how clean and neat he kept everything in the house. My mother told her sister that she was supposed to keep things up for living there, but that there was little for her to do. He enjoyed a clean house and if he saw as much as a dirty dish, he would wash it and put it away.

J. Michael Woods

**Billy and Mom (me in utero)
in front of Mr. Peacock's House**

Chapter Four

THE REVEALING

I went to visit my mother who had moved to Georgia with her husband Larry, whom she had married after the sad and untimely death of Robert Graham Reid Sr. I would receive two more sisters from this marriage. After years of Cootie never telling me what I believed in my heart to be true, I devised a plan. I would wait for my brothers and sisters to go to bed, hoping that my mother would stay up, with it being my first night there for my brief visit. When all was quiet, I said to her, "Mother, I know Jack Woods is not my father." Her eyes widened, and her lips began to tremble. Through her tears she asked, "Who told you this, your grandmother?"

"No, ma'am, you just did. I wanted to see your reaction. I have wondered about this for a long time."

Just like twins who have never met each other, they instinctively know that there is someone else, and I have felt this about my real dad. Mom got up from her chair, sobbing and came over and hugged me. She was beset with emotion in that moment, I struggled to hear his name clearly from her. She either said Oren or Olan. At this juncture, it did not seem important. I now knew for sure that my feelings were correct. Still crying she told me, "Johnny, I am so sorry!" My heart went out to her, and I told her that I loved her and was so glad that she had given me birth. I told her some of what my grandmother had told me about her and Jack, but that she would never tell me right out that he was not my father. She would always say if there were any difference than what was on my birth certificate, "…only your mom would know for sure." I told her how sorry I was that for such a young adult, still a teenager, that she had to face such heartfelt, fearful years. She went on to say that timing, and a young girl's longing to be embraced and held for security led to my existence.

Mom continued explaining that my father did know about me and that I had been born having a few complications. She said that Jack would return to port from delivering the barges several times while she lived in the upstairs apartment she and Billy occupied provided by my birth-father.

Mom said, "Your father came to the hospital to see you and exclaimed, 'He sure is my son. Johnny looks so much like my daughter when she was born. He even resembles me in some old baby pictures when I was an infant.' Thinking you were his own child; Jack rented another apartment for me to live in while I was still carrying you. I was about six months along and needed to leave your father's house before his wife and daughter returned from Germany. Once Jack found out you were not his child, Honey, he wanted a divorce. He must have done some thinking and realized we had not been together for me to even be six months pregnant."

Mom told me my dad was a bit older than she was. He was kind and had a big heart. "I suppose," she said, "he is why I married an older man such as Robert Reid, when I did remarry. I needed someone to help me, and Billy. Bob, as he was called, genuinely loved me, Johnny," she added. "I knew that you were loved by my mother, and you loved her. I tried several times to get you back, but the two of you were inseparable. It just wasn't to be."

After a few minutes of silent contemplation, Mom confessed, "I know that what I did was not right, sleeping with another woman's husband. I want you to know that moment felt so right, but I knew it was wrong. Your father made me feel safe and protected. I longed for that." "Mom, don't beat yourself up." I remember saying to her, "It's not all your fault, Mom, it takes two to create a baby, and he also shares responsibility."

"Johnny," she said, "I know that you're religious, and probably think I am so bad." She started to cry again. This time I hugged her and said, "But God also had a say in this. Psalm 139 declares that God sees us in the dark. What you may think is a secret, He knows all about it. He says that He formed me in your womb. He gave me soul and body and all His works are wonderful. God says that He knew me before I was even born. Mom, God surely will overcome any wrong that happened that night. Even when we don't do things right, God does."

As I held Mom's hand, she listened intently, and realized *God had a purpose for me.* That purpose would be challenged by many moments of doubt. Having much time on the island to think about things, propelled me forward, as well as prompted me to reflect on the past again and again. My childlike faith was given support by reading Psalm 139 which says, "*I praise you, for I am fearfully and wonderfully made.*" At that moment, Psalm 139 gave comfort to my mother. It may seem unusual for a young man to have such vivid events to ponder. Perhaps if I had been living inland and attending school, I would not have been so introspective. I would have been involved in normal teen activities. Such was not the case, as these long periods of isolation gave rise to my searching mind.

Chapter Five

BETWEEN A ROCK AND A HARD PLACE

So, here we were, as mentioned in Chapter 2, approaching the island with great speed. Ever so slowly my grandfather pulled back on the throttle that would slow down the outboard motor. He stopped and quickly went to the stern of the boat to lift the engine forward so that the propeller was out of the water. The boat gently drifted to a sandy spot where it beached itself. We both climbed out over the side of the boat onto the shore. "Why are we here?" I asked. "Just came to check out things and to explore the lay of the land," Uncle Bill retorted.

As a boy soon to turn twelve, this was sure exciting and different. The island was void of any habitants and rocky in most places. It had what seemed to me two sides with a low-lying marshland in the middle. There was a North side and South side where trees, known as Australian Pines, grew. These trees are not indigenous to Florida. They were introduced to Central and South Florida, primarily along the east coast, in the 1800's for wind breaks and shade. Being salt tolerant, they were able to thrive, where many plants would not survive. The Australian pine grows between 5 to 10 feet each year. The fast growing of the trees became a problem in later years because they would push out other plants that were indigenous to Florida. These trees were originally found in Southeast Asia, Northern Australia, and in the Western Pacific Island region.[1] They will grow quickly along shorelines from seeds produced and then transported to many locations by way of moving water.

The trees were absent from the middle marshland due to their shallow root system. In this area, the ground was absent of rocks and the tree's shallow roots would pull out of the ground much too easily. I heard a whistle from Uncle Bill, which meant to come. He said, "I found what I was looking for." A man of few words, what I couldn't learn from Uncle Bill, I would soon learn from Cootie that he was planning a move to the island. We climbed back into the boat and shoved off the shore using an oar. The engine started and off we went, heading back to the car that had been parked next to a large schooner owned by one of my grandfather's friends. It had been moored in a deep offshoot designed for the large vessel. Incidentally, whenever this boat had its massive sails up, it reminded me of the big schooners used in battles fighting on the open sea in our country's fight for freedom. I would stand on the bow of the schooner and pretend to be John Paul Jones facing defeat in an open sea battle with British frigates in 1779. After suffering severe casualties from several of the cannons backfiring on board the vessel, Jones communicated this defiant message to the British Navy, *"I Have Not Yet Begun to Fig*ht."[2] Jones' reported words would later become the battle cry of the modern U.S. Navy.

For a boy who had rarely been in a boat, it was exciting to be speeding down the dredged waterway between the dikes back to where we had parked. Suddenly, the motor, running wide open, began to sputter. I had no idea why. Uncle Bill got up from his seat, and on his way back to the motor, he said, **"Take the Steering!"** He had gone back to switch over the gas line to another tank. Full of pre-teen adrenaline, I took over with novice experience. I thought, I've got this! The excitement was momentary. The boat started to turn ever so slightly toward the North dike. I turned the steering wheel, as I called it, a little to the left and the boat direction did not change a bit; I turned a little more, still nothing. This was happening in seconds. I envisioned the boat crashing against the rocks on the dikes. In panic, I turned the wheel sharply, fearing the worst. The boat went into a spin. Uncle Bill fell backward in the stern, just short of being forced over the side. We made a couple of tornadic circles with the outboard motor going into a high pitch sound. He got up and pushed me aside, grabbing the steering and pulling way back on the throttle to slow the boat. While doing so he yelled with a ghost looking face, **"What are you trying to do, kill us?"** My first big adventure on the water and to the island went quickly from joy to defeat. I guess you could say, I felt like a sunken boat, if indeed a boat had feelings. Thank God we didn't flip over and sink! I was to find out that outboard motors begin to flutter when they're running out of gas and the tanks have to be changed. More importantly, I was to learn that a boat does not turn like a car. This boat had cables that ran from the steering mechanism back to the engine. Most of these cables have slack in them and do not apply tension turning the outboard motor if given just a slight turn. However, I also learned that if one turned way too far, the boat motor would then quickly react to the tension being applied and turn the vessel's direction. Little did I realize the events taking place would be symbolic of my life as a teenager in the coming years. A life plagued with Grand Mal seizures and Statis Epilepticus. As the boat spun out of control, so would normalcy in life for me do the same.

Her Heart and the DESIRE to Give Up

I asked Cootie why we would be moving to the island. She responded, "In recent years life has been tough on all three of us. Do you remember Johnny, that I almost died from a heart attack just over three years ago?" "Yes, I remember that scary moment." "Do you remember also how I just wanted to give up sitting out under that oak tree?" "Man, oh man, do I! I couldn't sleep at night. I was only in the second grade." As I write this today, I remember vividly that conversation. I would lay there at night with a deep sadness, trying to relax from my busy day. I remember the thought of Cootie dying while I was sleeping was more than my young mind could handle. The trauma to my psyche would be great. I watched her sitting around with no desire to do anything. This exacerbated my over - whelming fear when going to sleep at night. As the feelings encased me, I would feel tears running down my cheeks and into my ears. After all the late-night struggle, I would finally zonk out, and the next thing I knew Cootie was calling me to get up for school. Cootie, before the heart attacks, had always been happy go lucky and full of energy, but now seemed to move slow and tired as she helped me color coordinate my clothes to wear that day.

For many months, walking home from school to 115 S. 21st Street, I walked eastward on Boston Ave towards the side yard of the house. I would see my dear Cootie just sitting there out in the yard. One day after hearing her defeated response when I asked her how her day had been, I retorted rather abruptly, "You are just a selfish old lady! What about me! You sit there waiting to die and you know you are my everything! Why are you so selfish?" This little eight-year-old boy ran into the house crying.

The next day, I was coming up Boston Ave. again and I did not see her in the yard. This put fear in my heart. When I got in the house, there Cootie was preparing chicken to fry for supper that night. *Oh, those were the days long before Shake N Bake could be bought at your local market.* She later explained to me calling her selfish, reminding her how much she meant to me, well, that got her up and out of her chair. Cootie realized she had purpose and someone to live for. She said," Child, now quit your worrying. Your old grandmother is back." And back she was, joy and all! My deep-seated depression began to subside, and I was able to go to sleep at night, after, of course, I had said my prayers. I was joyful that night and I told the Lord He had answered my prayer, Cootie was back! God had not taken her as I slept.

"Children between the ages of six and seven develop an understanding of death, in which a fear can arise. The medical term for this fear I was experiencing is Thanatophobia. With the recognition that death will eventually affect everyone, and that it is permanent and irreversible, the normal worry about the possible death of family members, or even their own death can intensify. In some cases, this preoccupation with death can become disabling."[3] In my case, losing Cootie would have been traumatic. Yes, I trusted in God, but the realization of Cootie being taken away was so vivid for a child coming to understand the permanency of death.

Symptoms of Thanatophobia may not be present all the time. In fact, one may only notice the signs and symptoms when and if they start to think about their death or the death of a loved one. In a later chapter I will talk about what God did for me when she was taken from this world.

His Back and the DEGREE of Giving Up

"Concerning your grandfather, you know what pride he takes in his work." Cootie said. I replied, "I know, '**A job worth doing is worth doing right, and if a person pays you \$2 for doing a job, then give the person \$3 worth of work.**' I have heard Uncle Bill say that many times."

"Yes, and you know that since my heart attacks a few years ago and the discs deteriorating in his back, he nor I are able to keep up doing what we once did." Cootie added that she told him years ago that while he was still able, he needed to invest some of the money he made from construction. She said that she had suggested he put some excess cash that was sitting in savings into buying some property over on the beach. This was in the late 40s and early 50s. She went on to say that since he was nine years younger than her, he thought of himself as invincible. "Oh, Hell, woman, I'm not ever getting old," he would always respond. At that time, he was well known for his craftsmanship in building, and was highly respected. I knew that examples of his work could be seen in Saint Lucie and other surrounding counties. In fact, he was sought after as far away as Jacksonville and Tallahassee, and down through South Florida. This cavalier attitude did not mirror what he was now experiencing. She paused for a moment and then added one thing more. "What made all this worse was that the plastering your grandfather was known for, the work he had so loved and invested in, was being overtaken and replaced by drywall. Coupled with his medical bills and mine, with little cash flow, things were made difficult."

I queried so much it was hard for her to get supper prepared. "Well, does this have anything to do with the men I saw coming into the house and taking away some of the tools of his trade? They also managed to take most everything he had in his shed." She explained to me that he used those things for collateral to borrow money in hopes that the work would improve. He had also had a recent relapse of nerve problems he had been fighting since being a soldier in France, during World War II. Cootie explained further that many problems extended from his war days. "This is also why your mother left home so young. In the days preceding the war, we would go dancing on the weekends. He would have a few drinks or beers, and I would have Coka Cola. You know, Johnny, how much I love to dance and as a young adult I would perform on stage for fun as a Flapper. It's what they called that type dancing in my early days. When your grandfather came back from the war with injuries, he had become addicted to medication." "What happened to him?" I asked. She told me that he and some of his platoon had been cut off by German soldiers in a mountainous area and that the days and nights were frigid. A few days later when they were able to reconnect with their larger group, it was discovered that his feet were showing signs of frostbite. He stayed somewhere in a hospital, being treated for his feet and bronchitis. It was at this point then, he became addicted. She thought that before doctors knew how addicting some pills were, that they would give out these pain pills as you would give out candy. I asked her, "Is this why he screams out at night sometimes while he's dreaming?" "Yes, Honey," she said.

"He saw and did things that he has tried to forget, but as you hear in the night, sometimes he still has bad dreams."

He shared with her a particular time when he had taken a French soldier behind some bushes and shot and killed him. The soldiers kept being shelled by German artillery, and it was discovered that this person was reporting their location back to the Germans. He was with the Americans but was also working with the enemy. "How did any of this affect my mother?" I asked. "When he came back from war Johnny, we know that it is advised that one should not drink alcohol and take medications. He was taking pills and drinking, which made him do things. That just wasn't like him!" I quickly asked, "Like what?" "Well, Honey, he made advances towards your mom." In my heart I was sick." So, is this why she left home?" Cootie dropped her head low, "In part, it was," I was stunned!

My Brain and the DEMAND to Give Up

Looking back at this time, as I write today, there were a lot of sensitive things being told to me which were difficult for a 12-year-old boy to absorb. These things were foreign to what I knew about my grandparents and my mother. The people I knew at this point in my life were loving towards one another and did not go out on weekends to dance and party. My mother seemed to love my grandfather in a daughterly way. He reciprocated as a good father figure. When Bob Reid, my mom's second husband, died of cancer, we were all living together on North 17th Street in the city of Fort Pierce, FL. That had been five years prior. Yes, I was only seven, but everything seemed right to me. To a child, five years seemed like an eternity. During my mother's hard times, my grandmother and grandfather were there for her. Over the years of growing up, this would generally be the case. Mom was also there to help as they grew older with health needs of their own, regardless of the miles between them, I observed love.

Unwanted News

Several days later, Cootie brought up the conversation again about moving to the island. She said, "You know the other day you were talking about why this may happen." I said, "Yes, I want to know." "I mentioned to you about your grandfather's health and mine collapsing, and how we are also struggling to make ends meet. Well, Honey, your school called the other day and said that they could no longer accommodate you with seizures, in the classroom. When I said our declining health issues, I was talking about you too." This drove a spear through my heart. The news so shocked me that I started to cry, "But why? I enjoy school." I was emotional as I spoke. "I have done nothing wrong to be kicked out of school. Look at my conduct grades," I said, as I frantically tried to defend myself. "I've received nothing but A's in that since I was in the 1st grade, and this is my fifth-grade year."

I felt sick and sad. My grandmother told me that I had been a good boy, and that I wasn't being punished, but that the seizures I had suffered the week before in class had frightened all the children. Several of them had been told by their parents to stay away from me. I was to learn that epilepsy came with a negative societal stigma.

"So, is this about the recent seizure I had in the classroom?" She said, "Yes, and also about the one that you had on your bike after school." I had no memory of what happened during the seizure at school, but the other one I was conscious that something happened. I had crashed my bicycle while riding it home, but why?

Cootie explained that a man had seen me lying in the ditch and had come down to see what was wrong. I did not know how long I had laid there, but the man woke me from sleep. My tongue was bitten and there was blood all over the front of my shirt. I assumed I had hurt myself when I crashed into the ditch. I had told this man when he woke me up that I'd been riding home from my school, *Saint Anastasia*. He called the school about finding one of their students who wrecked his bike. He also told them that the boy seemed disoriented. "The following day is when the school called and asked if it was you. I had to tell them yes, Honey. We are supposed to meet with them next week to withdraw you."

My seizures had worsened from first grade when, as I said, I would get dizzy and see stars. By the 3rd grade, that first type had stopped, and a new type had begun. The teacher, Mrs. Livingston called on me to read. When I didn't answer her, she walked over to me and thought that I had zoned out. My lips were fluttering. This must be, she thought to herself, a new type of seizure activity. I was escorted many times to the office that school year. Off to the side was a small room which had a cot in it. I would lay down and stay quiet when these episodes would take place. Soon I would be able to get back into the routine of the day. This new type of seizure would come on without warning, and mostly I would not know what was going on around me. There was no flailing with my arms, just staring off into the air, oblivious to everything.

There were those rare exceptions, I remember one vividly, walking from class out to the bike rack. By the time I got there, something happened. I wasn't thinking clearly. The bike had a combination lock, and I was not able to remember what the numbers were to unlock it. All these years later, what I couldn't do that day, I am remembering now. The combination was to turn the dial twice past zero, then right to 6, then back left to 24, and finally back right to 7. Repeatedly, I had tried, but No Luck! Everyone had gone home for the day, so I just sat there by the bike rack. I was feeling strange, kind of like that feeling you get just before you are going to throw up. I could see that I was all alone, but I didn't really think about how I could go get help. I was totally focused on the lock. Suddenly Uncle Bill showed up. Cootie had sent him looking for me when he came home from work around 5:30. I can remember how tender he was toward me when he found me. Getting out of the truck he asked, "What are you trying to do, boy? Well, it's all OK. I'm here now." He easily dialed the combination, picked up my bike and put it in the truck. Now I was feeling safe. I was whisked home where Cootie wrapped her arms around me. She fed me some supper and I went to bed early. The next day I stayed home from school, but I felt great.

At this time in my life, I was taken to the J Hillis Miller Science Center in Gainesville, FL. After running some tests, doctors asked my grandparents a startling question, "What kind of accident has this young boy had? There are indications of scar tissue on parts of his brain. The markings on John's X ray show this. Furthermore, the EEG's show abnormal electrical activity." My grandparents reported some of the health issues that I had experienced since birth, especially the two poisonings at ages two and three. Ingesting the varnish was most likely the culprit.

There were few drugs at that time for seizure control. Dilantin had been invented in 1908 and became widely used in the 1940's. Doctors felt the continuation of Dilantin and Phenobarbital would be best for the present, even with their potential side effects. They also suggested trying to experiment with some things in my diet, including avoiding fried foods. Unfortunately, this made minimal, if any, difference in what my epileptic brain was doing.

The next week came all too quickly. The hurtful day we were to meet with school personnel was upon me. What would be said? How would I withstand this rejection? I quietly prayed out in the backyard before getting ready to go.

"Dear God, will you please help me this day?
And will you...?"
God did not answer the way I had hoped,
but He did hear.

I put on my church clothes, as I called them, to help myself feel better.

When arriving, all the students were gone from the classrooms and halls. While we waited for Mrs. McLaughlin, I slipped out to use the bathroom.

Memories flooded my mind of the many times I had used the boys' room over the years since first grade. There stood the urinals side by side. Over to my right were the stalls with commodes. I thought, how many times when having to use the commode, even if my stomach ached, how I would wait until there was no one in there to hear me go. Most boys didn't seem to care about passing gas and laughing as they did so. I, however, was private about these things, even though I knew everyone uses the bathroom. I think my teachers understood and would always allow me this time. I find it amazing what teachers intuitively know, as I think and write about this today. It's odd the feeling one has, even about a bathroom, if something is thought to be the last time.

The principal walked in just after I had returned. She was a tall, stately woman whose coif, which she always sported, seemed to be taller on her forehead than others I had seen. With her was Mrs. McLaughlin and Sister Josephenine. This Sister had been my 1st grade teacher, and I also had her for catechism and math in 2nd, 3rd, and 5th grades. She was a person who enjoyed having fun but was serious about teaching. She would drill the subject being taught until you could remember it flawlessly.

**LOVE is like SUGAR;
it blunts the bitter.**
J. Michael Woods

The principal had my things from my desk. As she handed them to me, she said, "John, we are so sorry for you to leave, but the seizure you had in class was much worse than any we have ever witnessed. The other children were very worried about you and concerned parents have called asking about this episode you experienced." She remained unemotional while speaking to me. She even commented on how nice I looked. Sister John Bride went on to explain how public schools usually provided a homebound teacher in situations like mine. She explained that she would talk more to my grandparents about this type of instruction and inform them who to call. The other teachers were wiping tears from their eyes, and this included stern Sister Josephenine." John," she said, "we are so sorry!" They hugged me and said they would pray for me. This was hard, but *it was cushioned by their expressed love.* I went out with my grandparents and got into Uncle Bill's truck. As he started the engine Cootie said, "Why don't we go down to Burger King and get a bite to eat? And, Johnny, you can have a Coke." So, off we went with one chapter ending in my life and a new one about to begin.

Chapter Five Endnotes

1. *gardeningsolutions.ifas.ufl.edu/care/weeds*
2. *historycollection.com*
3. *www.Americanacademyofpediatrics.org*
4. *www.healthychildren.org*
5. www.healthline.com/health/Thanatophobia

Chapter Six

THE NEW WORLD

Immigrants came looking for a beginning and to escape persecution that they had been experiencing. They referred to this land across the ocean as New. This name was first coined much earlier by the explorer, Amerigo Vespucci. He called it Mundus Novus – Latin for "new world." In 1507, German mapmaker, Martin Waldseemüller published a book on geography. In this book, he referred to Vespucci's hemispheric find as "America" in honor of the explorer. While Vespucci continued to call the lands Mundus Novus, the name America stuck and entered into everyday use in European circles. Being a mapmaker, Waldseemuller knew the feminine gender was employed when naming continents, thus Amerigo became America.[1]

My grandfather had been searching out a new plot of land across from the mainland of Saint Lucie County, Florida. He was looking to alleviate financial woes, and to escape to a more simple lifestyle. The early pioneers going West in this new land would have said during a time of threat, "Let's circle the wagons." Uncle Bill was trying to protect what he had left and make life's troubles manageable. *I remember the philosophy of the famous Mr. Rogers, "Anything mentionable, is manageable."* While not responsible for the phrase, his beloved friend and mentor Margaret McFarland actually spoke the words, yet Rogers made it his primary focus.[2] Moving to the island had been mentioned and explored and Uncle Bill felt like it was now manageable, especially so, since each of us had been severed from our mainland identities. Uncle Bill did not have employment and Cootie's health had plummeted. I was left with being barred from school because of the grip of epileptic seizures taking a tighter hold to my body and life.

Gathering the Essentials

Uncle Bill had done some work for our longtime neighbors, the Lloyds. With the money he received from them, he purchased a large blue camping tent and some oil lanterns. He also purchased a Coleman camping stove that operated using a small gas filled tank. This came with two burners, and the tank had to be primed with air to burn hot. The flame would get smaller as the air was used, making it necessary to repump air into the chamber if used for a period of time. Imagine how often this stove had to be primed while cooking a pot of beans or chili, etc. Along with this type of stove, there were several Coleman gas lanterns which would burn bright. They also had to be pumped full of air to force out the flame onto the filament. The filament was durable to withstand heat yet was fragile if handled or touched by an object. These would be used only on occasion since they burned fuel quickly. The kerosene lamp would burn slowly producing much less light and using less fuel. There was no house waiting for us when we made the move to this hopefully new beginning. What would also be new to me, and sad, was the loss of returning to school for the next seven years. There would be no high school graduation with my classmates in the future. Plus, I was even being cut off from seeing them with this move. I would especially miss Frank. We rode bicycles together and he had become like a brother to me. Over the years, he would be remembered as the best buddy ever, who would live large in my heart. At times I had protected him from bullies, and now, he was protecting me, keeping me from being friendless, with fond memories that would bring me comfort as the years passed. But God in His sovereignty would cause our paths to cross briefly several more times in the future.

Assembling and Building

The first day on the island, I busied myself helping Uncle Bill level the ground where the tent would be set up. We had to have the tent standing and secured before nightfall, since it would be needed for protection from the elements while we were sleeping. The tent had a plastic like liner for the floor. We would all sleep on cots which were folded up and put out of the way during the day. My grandparents would sleep on one side with cots side by side, and I, on the other side. It was supposed to be rainproof, but, well you guessed it, during a down pour it would leak all over. With no electricity, there was also no running water. Water was brought over from the mainland in old used gallon bleach bottles, in quantities of about 20 bottles at a time. Fresh water from these bottles was used sparingly. We would catch rainwater for my grandmother to wash her hair. We poured water into a small white basin to wash our bodies. Uncle Bill had built an outhouse out of plywood and two by fours. This was put away from our living quarters. It was small and could be lifted by him and me to move it when needed. It sat over a large hole in the ground that I had dug. Lime was used to reduce unpleasant odors. I often left the door open for maximum fresh air. No electricity, true, but what I had was an all-natural, air-conditioned bathroom, when needed.

There was an immediate need for a dock to be put in, so we could tie and moor our boat. This would make it possible to get out of the 16ft. boat onto dry land, missing the water and the shore's wet sand. Until the dock was in place, we would secure the boat using a grapple anchor and row to the shore using a lightweight aluminum boat that could be pulled up onto the island. Uncle Bill would go out about on the island choosing the straightest Australian pine for the dock piling.

I learned how to use an axe and to make a tree fall in the desired direction by cutting a notch. After cutting them, the

> **I thought of myself as the mythical Paul Bunyan.**

felled trees would then be trimmed and one by one transported to where they would be used. I would take down many a tree by axe in the coming years. I thought of myself as the mythical Paul Bunyan. This would give me tremendous upper body strength, along with pushing wheel barrels full of rocks. The island had many rocks to contend with. Pathways and our ever-enlarging yard required clearing and making it level and smooth. I would take these rocks, dump them, and eventually over the years, make a type of jetty that would help in keeping the shore we used most from washing away. It was to make a good current break and a good spot for fishing in later years.

The House Uncle Bill built

We lived in the tent for just over a year until Uncle Bill would have the money to build a small two room house, again from plywood and two by fours. The floors were secured to a concrete and block foundation. He used lots of rebar to add strength. I would mix the concrete using barrels of accumulated rainwater as needed to blend with white sand that was absent of any other solid substance. The two room structure had a plywood roof with tarpaper sealing it, and later was covered with shingles. This was all hard work, but I enjoyed helping my grandfather.

The Sandflies and the Priest

One day while we were still living in the tent, the sand flies were again being ferocious. Mosquitoes were bad each night, especially at first light and at sunset just before dark. With trees being trimmed and overgrowth contained or removed, this kept the mosquitoes down during the day. Sand flies or sandfleas, as the northerners referred to them, only came out at certain times. Moonlit nights, rain and certain eastern winds seemed to be when they came in droves. I remember on one occasion; Cootie was trying to cook outside the tent using the Coleman stove. The sand flies had been bad for several days. Suddenly, my grandmother yelled and proclaimed, "These damn piss ants flying around! I wish they would get out away from here!" She swatted and danced around rubbing them from her arms and legs.

As I looked over at her from where I was reading, in my startled moment I said, "Cootie, you don't talk like that." "Honey," she said. "I'm sorry, but these things are getting on my last nerve." I went over and covered her arms and legs with rubbing alcohol. It had a eucalyptus smell, and I knew it was good for taking away the sting of bites, as well as repelling some insects. As she sat down to rest awhile, she said, "This brings back memories of Fort Pierce Beach at the beginning of World War II." "What about the beach?" I asked.

Naval Amphibious Training Base

"Well," she said, "before your grandfather was drafted in the war, and throughout the dark years it was raging, the beach was turned into an amphibious base, training special spies and scouts for the military. There were rumors in town that some of the young boys training over there had shot themselves due to the onslaught of the sand flies. They sometimes, as you know, are around for days. Over on the beach, with all the sand, they can be even worse." "That's horrible!" I spoke. I had not known about the beach being used as the training place for special military projects.

"Yes, and the beach had been closed to the public. Only military were allowed over there." "Wow!" I said, "right here in Fort Pierce." She said, "I think they closed the beach to everyone around 1942. Most people were kept off, but you know your grandfather, he knew secret ways for getting over there. Growing up on this river, he knew the cuts and waterways very few knew. He could secretly get over there using these and bypass all the known ways. He could do this fully undetected."

Clergy Goes Bump in the Night

Cootie went on, "This reminds me of the night Uncle Bill, and his brother Jerome and I were up in the cuts fishing. Your Uncle Bill said to his brother, 'Listen, did you hear that? Sounds like oars hitting against the side of a boat.' You know what alert and keen hearing he has." "What was happening?" I asked. She answered, "It was someone coming in a boat. It was 1:30 in the morning. They thought, who could that be? They quickly got behind a cluster of large mangroves and waited in the dark. It was pitch black that night with no moonlight. Suddenly, there went a boat slowly going by. To our surprise, it was a priest from my Catholic Church." "What?" I asked. "Yes, and he nearly bumped into us, Johnny. He had all kinds of candles like the ones you light in honor of someone in church. He even had several racks that were used to hold the candles. Your Uncle Bill and Jerome were determined to find out what he was up to. They took me in the boat, staying quiet and far behind so as not to alert him. Johnny, child," she said, "He took those candles way up in the Australian pine trees. You know those tall, swaying ones just north of the inlet? And he lit them." "What was he doing?" "Well, since the beach was used for special military projects, we thought he was giving a signal out in the ocean to someone. They decided to leave and report this to the base commander as soon as they could send a message stating they needed to speak with him ASAP!"

"What happened next?" I asked excitedly! "They were escorted to a meeting and reported what they had witnessed. He asked them, 'What are you two guys trying to pull? A priest would not be doing something like this. Get out of here!' He acted at the time like he didn't believe them, but a few days later German submarines were blown up in the Atlantic Ocean north of Fort Pierce. Their supplies washed ashore. Many food products were labeled *Made or Grown* in Fort Pierce, FL. We figured that they were needing food and supplies being so far away from Germany, way across the ocean. When these submarines surfaced briefly, men would most likely come over in row boats when they saw the signal in the trees at night."

"Why would he want to help them?" I had to understand. "The only explanation that your grandfather could think of is that the priest's parents were living in Germany. He, being of German descent, and having parents still residing there, was probably threatened by the German Gestapo, their secret police. They most likely promised to kill his parents if he did not aid them and cooperate. You know, we believed that they had their tentacles everywhere." "This is so sad," I said. Cootie went on to say, "Nothing happened to the priest that we know of, just the submarines were destroyed. I think I hear your grandfather's boat coming.

Go see if you can help him and carry some of those water jugs. You sure helped me with those pesky sandflies."

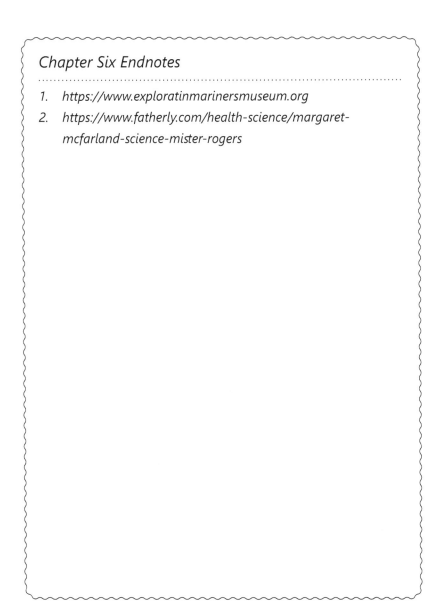

Chapter Six Endnotes

1. *https://www.exploratinmarinersmuseum.org*
2. *https://www.fatherly.com/health-science/margaret-mcfarland-science-mister-rogers*

MEMORIES SHROUDED WITH THE THREAT OF WAR

I turned twelve that first year on the island. Seizures were happening about twice a month and growing in intensity. Walking along on the other side of the island, I realized I needed to stay away from the water, to honor Cootie's wishes. She told me to go into the water, only if she or someone else was with me. I kept my ear tuned to her call, remarking to myself, "Sure is hard for a boy to stay away from the water when he is surrounded by it." The water was so inviting! A soft breeze whispered its way through the pines. In the distance, the seagulls were making their usual squawking sound. Normal communication between them was noisy, but this time there were five or six bickering over a fish and they were squealing. The tone reminded me of the mocking I had endured from a circle of boys due to my speech impediment. It had improved quite a lot since then and I was happy about that. I knew Frank was a sincere friend, because he never joined in or made fun of the way I spoke; as did many of the boys. Also, girls did not seem to have the need to pick on someone who had a vulnerability.

Going back in time, I cherished another female in my life who showed me a lot of love and care, besides my grandmother, my sister Rose Marie. Yes, almost three years younger than me, she stood with me and for me.

When we were in second and third grade, she had lived with us part of that school year. I could not have any water to drink after 7:00 PM each night. My grandparents felt this would aid me in not wetting the bed as I slept. It had become frustrating and embarrassing for me, having to contend with such an albatross of an event.

I remember waking up in the morning with my first thought being, *"Did I wet the bed?"* I would feel around on the bed and sadly, my hand would deliver the message of wet sheets. **"Why, dear God"** I would ask? *"You know that I pray every night going to bed that I won't."* I was never punished for wetting the bed. Parents should realize that children do not exhibit bed wetting on purpose. For me personally, it was probably due to my medications that would put me into a deeper sleep than most children experience. There is always a reason, and not a moral one which can be corrected by punishing the child. Occasionally my sister would wake up and climb down the ladder from the top bunk, while I slept on the bottom. She would whisper, "Johnny, wake up and go to the bathroom." I was made to sleep on the bottom bunk due to any seizure activity that may occur.

Besides waking me in the night, Rose Marie would try to slip me some water in my little blue Captain Kangaroo cup. Marie would say, "There is nothing wrong with a smidgen of cold water to cool your lips." A taste would be just enough. She would also say, "Just open your mouth when you are taking your nightly shower and gulp in some water. Uncle Bill and Cootie will never know." I answered, "But, God would know! This would be disobeying them, and to do it would be to sin against God." She looked up at me with a determined face and said, "Johnny, just shut up and do it; God will understand." Did I ever do it? Occasionally, yes, but I would feel so guilty. *The flesh always desires and longs for things when it is told, Thou Shalt Not Have.*

Crisis at the Border

It was October, 1962, a couple years before my grandparents and I moved to the island. The Cuban Missile Crisis was taking place and we were having drills at school. We would get down in front of our desks with our faces toward the floor and our hands over our eyes. We were told the bright light from the blast could blind us if it hit close by. Russia had placed nuclear missiles in Cuba only 90 miles off the coast of Florida's most southern point; the Keys.[1] Confrontation between Russia and the United States was imminent. I remember watching military vehicles for several days, one after another, travelling down Virginia Ave. which ran beside our house. This road was known as a feeder to the Florida Turnpike, or in the eastward direction, a feeder to US 1, which was our main way of traveling north or south besides the Turnpike in those days.

Because I prayed daily, and talked about God a lot, Rose Marie said to me with a frightened face, "Johnny, I don't want to die, being blown up."

Recognizing her sincere fear, I said to her in my childlike trust, simple and pure, "It's OK if we die, God promises that when we die, we go directly to Him, and we will live forever with Him and his angels." She grabbed hold to my shirt, pulling me close, and said, **"You don't understand, I want to live my life**! I love my life, and I am not ready to die." She abruptly left the room. To help block out some of her worries, Rose Marie could often be heard singing the early Beatles' songs, which celebrated life and love. With the preparation drills at school and parents sitting around discussing the grave possibilities, is it any wonder the children were on edge? Looking back on this occasion and how my innermost trust in God was shared with my sister many years ago, I recognize this truth.

Regardless how old we get, or what we face in life, we can rest assured that Satan will use every opportunity to take advantage of our fear and doubt. He wants to destroy our faith in the Lord. However, God always has a plan, and brings us comfort in all situations.

Chapter Seven Endnotes

1. *https://www.history.com/news/cuban-missile-crisis-timeline-jfk-khrushchev*

BUGS AND DINOSAURS

Not being able to explore the water as I would have wanted, led me to spend time exploring the topography of the island. Here, I would discover bull ants and Black Widow spiders, along with many different size bones. I would watch and wonder how insects could have gotten over here, since salt water was not conducive to their survival. Over time, I would learn that these and other insects would come across from the mainland catching a ride on debris that would eventually wash up on the shoreline. The ants would be living under rotting limbs on the ground from the pines, and the spiders would be under the multitude of rocks, of all sizes, which covered most of the landscape. Needing to entertain myself, having no one to play with, I began to pretend that I was playing war, having battles with the invasive bull ants and the poisonous widow spiders who were known for killing the male after mating.

Soldier Boy

Besides the boy inside of me wanting to play, there was also a war going on in Vietnam. Lyndon Johnson had become president after the brutal and sad assassination of John F Kennedy. Johnson won the general election held in November of 1964 and continued as president.[1] He deployed ground troops to Southeast Asia in 1965, the same year we moved to the island. I would go around the area looking for critters with whom to battle. At the time, I did not comprehend, nor did I appreciate their value to the ecosystem. Captivated by the explosions and gunfire heard only over the radio because we could not use a television without electricity, my imagination would wander. War games became me acting out what I imagined. I would decimate the enemy ants when I discovered them hiding under tree limbs or pine needles. The big cache would be to locate main nests and obliterate them. On other days, I would go out on patrol looking for the Vietcong, which were deadly and fierce. I read in the (mullet wrapper,) referring to what local fishermen called the Fort Pierce News Tribune, about the Vietcong. They were a network of communist sympathizers and fighters in South Vietnam. They were irregular soldiers, supported by the government of North Vietnam, located in the city of Hanoi, North Vietnam's capital. It was later renamed Ho Chi Minh City, in recognition of the President of the North, when the bloody Civil War ended.

Weapons: Self-Made and Toxic

During the war, the Viet Cong employed effective tactics by using booby traps. Some of these were known as the deadly Punji Sticks. Unaware of their impending doom, the opposing soldiers would step on them in a hole often covered with brush. The Vietcong were ingenious in employing these lethal and sharpened bamboo sticks. Laying the sticks side by side, they would link them together, using various methods that would severely injure the soldier. Trapdoors were sometimes made from punji sticks. Using a tripwire, these doors, hidden away, were made to snap up engaging the soldier to fall into, and often be stabbed to death when making contact. To make things more deadly, and infect the noted target with bacteria, they would often smear excrement on the sharpened tips.[2] One can almost hear these guys laughing as they applied their waste and readied the trap. Other weapons were grenade and snake pit traps, where poisonous snakes were transferred to places troops would dive into or behind during a surprise attack.

In my world, they were represented by the vicious widow spider, which has a bite that will severely affect a person's nervous system, even killing them in rare cases. With only audible sounds coming from the portable Zenith AM and FM radio, during the first three years on the island, the sounds of war were anything but quiet. They were animated in my young and waiting mind yearning for action. I would repeat the sounds I had heard as I battled the ants and spiders, which I dubbed the enemy while playing and entertaining myself. Picking up rocks of various sizes, with each one being a different weapon, I would make the appropriate sound as the make-believe weapons were shot or released as bombs. There were helicopters and jets called in for backup. I liked launching rockets and dropping a payload right on top of the enemy whenever the ground troops called for such help. The ants, the regular army of the North, would scatter looking for another place to hide. The widow spiders, designated the Cong, would hide under rocks. As the ground troops carried out a search and destroy mission, rocks would be overturned to reveal the hiding places of these spiders. The spiders would insert themselves deep into the crevice of a rock making them sometimes hard to root out. Special weapons had to be used to reach them. Not only would they hide deep inside the crevice of the rock, but often had an escape route as well. They would somehow recognize that they were in real danger and would use a furrow leading to another hideaway connected to the first.

As an adult, information I came across in my readings, supported the idea that my imagination as a young boy was typical. Michael Gurian refers to this in his book, *The Wonder of Boys*. He explains that due to brain development and testosterone, boys are hard wired to turn things into weapons more often than girls. His analysis of how boys learn and develop is a thoughtful read. I found his explanation informative of how a boy's brain develops compared to a girl's. It gives a plausible answer as to why most boys are more physical in communication and girls are more verbal in their interactions.[3]

Comparing widow spiders to the Vietcong was also more accurate than I could have imagined at my age. The VC had many tunnels built underground in the South region of the war. They used them to move supplies undetected, and to escape to another hiding place, just as the widow spiders used the tiny pathway from one crevice to another under the rocks. My imagination was to play a strategic part in my learning as the years went by. I scouted out the land picking up rocks and playing war games only to discover an unusual find of bones and teeth. Showing these finds to my grandfather, he agreed that they were bones and teeth, but of what? I suspended many of my war games, and instead started to explore, giving my new activity a name, Seek and Find. Little did I realize how seek and find would become related to scripture in the not-too-distant future.

Seeking Answers

At times, the seizures had interrupted my war games, as they sometimes did during my search and query of the bones and teeth I had found. After many months and dozens of finds, we took them to the University of Florida at Gainesville, while having yet another visit there concerning my epilepsy and the problem developing. The paleontologist we spoke with at the science geological department concerning fossils and bones, identified what had been found. Of these bones that we had taken for identification, he explained, various historic animals had been found. They were identified as mammoth and mastodon bones along with several 1/2 pieces of their large teeth. If these are only half, they must have been huge, I thought. They were about four inches in width and five inches in height. One could see what looked like where the roots of the teeth fastened into the gums and jawbone. Camel teeth and saber - tooth tiger teeth were identified along with horse teeth. Many different bones of these animals were also identified. These, we were told, were in the middle of the Indian River Lagoon, and must have been pumped up when creating the Spoil Island, deepening the main channel. The paleontologist explained that many different animals had lived in Florida at one time and that Florida is like an oasis in a belt region of the earth where deserts are found. It is also thought that Florida was once a part of Africa. The paleontologist suggested that as the area suffered drought conditions, sink holes developed swallowing up animals as they roamed. Quite possibly there was a drinking hole attracting the animals to that spot. As the fresh water dried up, the animals went further out to drink, sinking down in the mud, unable to get out.

I thought, Wow, what an education! I am only going to school three hours a week. I am almost always on the island away from regular school and people, but I am learning things that I most likely would never have learned in a regular school setting.

In later years, I would learn about Maria Montessori. She was the first female graduate in medicine in Italy. Montessori was an assistant doctor at the psychiatric clinic of

> **Education cannot be effective unless it helps a child open himself up to life.**
> Maria Montessori

the University of Rome. During this time, she had noticed school age children who were roaming the streets. She found that they were mostly from low-income families who were unable to afford schooling. Called Casadei Bambini, the school for little ones opened in an apartment building in Rome in 1907. She believed that a child could learn from simple beginnings by tackling concepts that employed all their God given senses. She developed manipulatives for students to help instruct them and further their learning ability. Montessori included things such as personal care, sweeping, and cleaning. When teaching about the environment, Montessori took the students outside for a firsthand look. She saw the role of the teacher as being one of facilitator, who could move about and create a safe environment in which the children could learn. This was so much better for them than being on the street. Montessori's methods eventually became known worldwide, giving children concrete experiences while moving them toward the abstract.[4] On the island, I lived in a controlled environment and developed a learning style that would propel me throughout life. Learning of Maria Montessori's methods was a good, unexpected finding.

Chapter Eight Endnotes

1. www.whitehouse.gov/about-the-white-house/presidents/lyndon-b- johnson

2. thevietnamwar.info/punji-sticks

3. Michael Gurian. The Wonder of Boys. (New York: Jeremy P. Tarcher/Penguin/Penguin Group USA Inc., 1996, 2006) 6-14

4. https://amshq.org/.../Who-Was-Maria-Montessori

Chapter Nine

MRS. COFFEY AND HER BOOKS

I began my homebound experience at age thirteen. One day while she was in town, my grandmother took the advice given to her about checking with St. Lucie County Schools. It had been an insurmountable task convincing my grandfather of this need I had for schooling. He envisioned me getting some type of trade if my epilepsy improved. He viewed a high school diploma as something, frankly, out of reach. Cootie needed to be persuasive and creative at the same time. Since she could not drive, we would need Uncle Bill to take us. We also needed a house where the homebound teaching could take place three hours each week.

She said, "You know, Bill, you can run your errands during this time. Just drop Johnny and me off at your mom's house. Thankfully, she's allowing us to come. I can invite Gladys over from next door and the three of us can visit on the front porch while Johnny studies awhile."

There would be more obstacles to overcome, but with his Okay, I enrolled as a sixth-grade homebound student. It was for me, like mission control at the Nasa Space Program after hurdles were overcome in launching.

"... 3, 2, 1 ignition! We have liftoff of the Apollo Spacecraft" I heard many times on the radio. Back then, I would go to the north part of the island and watch the spacecrafts as they soared south southeasterly with the sunlight reflecting off them. Eventually, they would disappear into space, overcoming earth's gravity. These Apollo Spacecraft missions were in operation from the early 60's into the 70's. They were rife with tragedies and triumphs. The worst tragedy occurred in 1967, when a fire broke out and the three-man crew perished on board at the launching pad. The greatest of NASA's triumphs was the fulfilling of the will of former President John Kennedy and America, by being the first and only country to land a crew on the surface of the moon, before the 1960's drew to a close.

I too, was on a mission. My ship was not full of fuel, but full of trust in the God who made space, earth, and all that inhabits them. Yes, God had answered my prayer concerning going to 6th grade, if only for a few hours each week. *He did not answer the way I expected, but I found that God had met my needs.* I would meet with Mrs. Coffey on Tuesdays and Thursdays. She made a huge difference in my life as she satisfied my yearning for learning in academic areas. Meeting with her would also launch me from my solitude on the island to weekly socialization.

The day started early, and all seemed to go well until we got to the old Ford Econoline waiting for us, parked on the mainland. The boat had started on the second turn of the ignition. There was no rain or wind, and the sun was shining brightly. It was a perfect day until we reached the truck and the three of us were seated. As Uncle Bill turned the key, the engine engaged a couple times, hesitating to start. "OH, no!" I said to myself. I had heard that sound before. This time however it was not the battery, but the carburetor. Uncle Bill raised the engine hood that set inside the vehicle between the two front seats. He retrieved the gas can from the boat and poured a small amount of gasoline into the carburetor. I thought, "What if the truck caught fire just as I was blasting off for homeschool?" Recently, Apollo 1 had burst into flames. I feared our old Ford Econoline would do the same because of trouble with its carburetor. It controlled fuel vapor and I knew Apollo in part exploded due to fuel vapors. But this was not that day, "Hot dog!" my heart felt as I heard the engine start. We were again on our way. After this slowdown, I sure was glad that Uncle Bill liked to get to where he is going early, because we arrived in the nick of time.

My instruction was to begin at 9:00 am. Mrs. Coffey was already there. She stood up from the table and introduced herself. She was a tall, stately woman with a southern accent. That first session on Tuesday was taken up doing several things. She wanted me to tell a little about myself and express my feelings about homebound school. In return, Mrs. Coffey told me a little about herself. She had been raised in Georgia, a little south of Greensboro. After teaching several years, she moved and taught school in Florida. She told me she had been teaching homebound for a long time. "Your grandmother tells me that you thoroughly enjoy learning. I thoroughly enjoy teaching, so we should get along simply fine, "she said as she smiled. I told her that my mother was born in Greensboro, GA. and that I had family there by the name of Moon. My mother's dad was Robert C. Moon, and his brothers and sister were Virgil, Harry, and Ruth. She leaned forward with eyes wide open and said, "Ooo, John, that's remarkably interesting. Now, perhaps, we should get started."

Mrs. Coffey showed me the textbooks she had brought, addressing each subject needed for the 6th grade. The books were used, but to me they were beautiful. They had that certain smell that one who reads a lot can recognize. Next, she handed me a syllabus of all the requirements for that month. She explained to me that I would need to be doing most of this work at home. I should read and study a lot and complete any written work at home on the island. She stated that most of her limited time with me would be teaching the subject matter and grading completed work. She needed to grade my work to ensure understanding and give herself opportunity to reteach if necessary. She told me to make note of any questions I may have. Before I knew it, the session was over. In my arms I held books, but to me they were as windows. It has been said that reading is a window to the world. Being on that island, I needed those windows from which to peer out.

My 6th grade school year was a tremendous success. I excelled at rocket speed. Speed had become a commodity during World War II, as the military quickly transported troops and supplies where needed and eventually defeated Germany and Japan. With the Air Force becoming its own military branch in September of 1947, along with Chuck Yeager breaking the sound barrier as early as October of 1947, speed was a societal buzz word among the public.

To satisfy the public's thirst created by speed, the Chevrolet Corvette made its debut in 1953, with more popular models making the line-up over the years. The Ford Thunderbird was first sold in 1955. Even its name projected the word speed. The Ford Mustang by 1964 was a widely desired car, being compact and fast. Not to be outdone, was the Chevrolet Camaro with the Z28 model having style and speed, fascinating the public. My reserved, laid-back cousin, Steve, was drawn to the thrill of this fast-moving car.

Fast found its way into the kitchen. First, primarily commercial ovens termed *Radar Range* came out in 1946. By the early 60s, they had become known as the microwave oven, with the '67 kitchen countertop model becoming a quick way to prepare food for a people who had become fast moving in many of their ways. Microwave ovens led to many in society wanting things done with microwave speed.

Island life was a dichotomy from life on the mainland. My life's world was slow, and now as a teenager, I was like a fast car idling in neutral, with my motor revving at high levels of RPM, yet not moving. My prayer had been that getting to be homeschooled, I would gain some traction and move forward in seeing my dreams come true. Whatever they were, I knew it would involve being educated. Where all this would lead, I did not know for certain, but God had put within me a quest to consume books, especially His book, the Bible. It brought me more comfort than any other. God's Word was teaching me that I was not a forgotten mistake, but a work in progress.

In 1975, Bill Gaither would pen the song, "I am a Promise, I am a Possibility." I remember thinking how well that phrase expressed my feelings from the island days in the 60s and 70s. In fact, as I write today in  2021, I had to stop and listen to the song being sung once again by the Gaither Trio. Yes, being homeschooled had given me some normalcy and a feeling that my nightly prayers were being heard by God above. Could it be that He was guiding my steps for the future even on the island? The school year was coming to an end Mrs. Coffey said, "See you for 7th grade; your 6th grade year has been a great success and it has been my pleasure to have been your teacher."

Over the summer between 6th and 7th grade, I had restudied the coursework, just as a matter of reviewing and keeping it all in my head. My grandparents had been informed that the days and time of the meeting would remain the same. I was again full of expectations. The summer had been filled with planting flowers with my grandmother and continuing to haul rocks off to create more area for our yard, which we leveled and smoothed for easy accessibility. I was now fourteen and Grand Mal seizures were happening with greater frequency and severity. I would bite my tongue, cheeks, and lips. Hydrogen peroxide was my constant companion, as it was useful in healing the bites I would make to my mouth and lips. Oh, how painful it was to bite up my mouth with my own teeth. The knots and bruises to my head and body were also becoming a reality, as a seizure would often take place with no warning, causing me to fall like a board into whatever.

Familiar words, But GOD...

The first day back with Mrs. Coffey had come. We were glad to see one another, but she also delivered some bad news concerning schooling. She said that due to upcoming budget cuts by the school system, this would be her last year to teach me. She said that she was sad to inform me and my grandparents of this news. She further said, "more than any of her students, she regretted telling me the most. However," she added positively, "I have an idea, and this is based on how well you understood the 6th grade curriculum."

She directed her comments toward my grandparents. "John can probably complete 7th and 8th grade requirements in one year. Mr. and Mrs. Jaudon," she went on. "If John is willing, and you are in agreement with this lofty but do-able plan, this will get him completely through with middle school." Uncle Bill spoke up, "I don't always understand this boy, but he does have the ability to work hard and also has a knack for book knowledge." Cootie piped in and said, "Johnny does read well. He uses words that I have never heard, and he has a wonderful way of explaining their meanings. I so much enjoy him reading the Bible to me and explaining it. You know there are words in there that I can't pronounce or understand."

"So, I guess it's a go," Mrs. Coffey said. "I was sure hoping it would be. I will bring his textbooks in so that John can peruse them with the 7th and 8th grade syllabus."

After I was given another arm-load of books, Mrs. Coffey left for that day. We went shopping for groceries after this, and Uncle Bill even suggested that we stop at McDonald's and get a Big Mac with a belly wash, referring to a Coke. Cootie ordered a single with

> **Behold, the LORD's hand is not shortened that it cannot save, nor His ear dull, that it cannot hear.**
> Isaiah 59:1 KJV

cheese and a cup of coffee. He asked her, "How do you drink that dishwater?" She answered him with, *"Well, not everyone was born with a tongue with perfect taste buds."* He looked at her and grinned.

The school year went quickly, and as was the plan, both 7th and 8th grades were completed. The one drawback was that this year was mingled with more seizure activity. On the last day I was to see Mrs. Coffey, she brought me all kinds of textbooks that had been discarded for newer versions by the high school. She wished me well and said she had enjoyed teaching a student so willing to learn. I gave her a hug and told her how much she meant to me. Years later, I am so thankful that she was another extension of God's hand in my life.

God was showing me how long His reach is, even to the middle of the Indian River Lagoon! His reach was to show me in the not-too-distant future how He intended to reach into my spiritual life as well as my physical. I am reminded here, of Ecclesiastes 4: 9-10. *Two are better than one, because they have a good reward for their toil. For if they fall, one will lift up his fellow. But woe to him who is alone when he falls and has not another to lift him up!"*

The words of poet, John Donne, (1572-1631) are reflected here.[1]

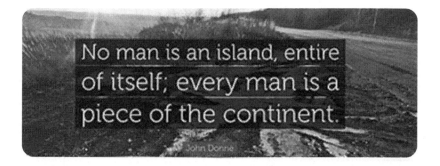

No man is an island, entire of itself; every man is a piece of the continent.

John Donne

Today we might say, no person is an island unto themselves, we are all a piece of one another. God has placed many people in my life who have played pivotal roles. I do not know where I would be without them. Nor do those that I have helped know where they would be today. I think it's safe to say, we all would be a whole lot less without the aid of others, especially the overshadowing aid of the Living God.

Chapter Nine Endnotes

1. *www.quotefancy.com*
2. *Inventions circa the 1940s to the 1970s may be easily researched via the internet.*

Chapter Ten

WHEN GOD SEEMS SILENT

Island Boy's dawn at age fourteen, would see psychological stormy days. The daunting days of seizures, loneliness, and depression would continue to bring threatening dark horizons, even as the sun was rising in the east. I can testify to you from firsthand experience that all three of the aforementioned truly hurt. *Yes, they all impair, but by using different modes to reach the central vein of hope.* I call those days evil because Satan seemed to have had a three-spirit tag team seeking to destroy me. None of these maladies are evil in and of themselves, however, *Satan will use any uncomfortable situation or trial to bring disarray, in his effort to rob one of hope.* Scripture identifies Satan as the father of lies.[1] Satan's Modus Operandi is confusion and fear. He begins his deceit with lies, just as he did with Eve in the Garden.

I found myself wondering sometimes if God had deserted me or even cared. Yes, here I was doubting after all God had already done. From birth to my early teens, He had done great things for me; I opined to self. Most recently, He had answered my heart's desire for continued

"To be helped and liked is to never be alone."
J. Michael Woods

education with an actual teacher, even if it was only a few short hours per week. Also, I had attempted 7th and 8th grade combined into one year and was successful. Mrs. Coffey had said, due to budget cuts, she would no longer be able to assist me. This was eerily like what I had been told in 5th grade. Different reasons were offered, but still the same effect. Once again, the schools were closing themselves to me. Their shutting doors seemed to shout, ***"You got past us for these two years, now we will be dead bolted!"***

This shout was to be fully repeated to me as Mrs. Coffey said her goodbyes, handing me yet more discarded books. "John," she said, "You have done remarkably well, and I will be sad not to see you for 9th grade. You have proven to me that you enjoy learning. Take these books, read and enjoy." I thanked her; never to see her again. She was to remain vivid in my memory.

The success of completing middle school was overshadowed with sad events, *but God!* The seizure activity, just before I turned 14, had intensified. I was now restricted even more as seizures plagued me. Imagine with me the fear of knowing that you're about to lose all sense of reality. Where was life about to take you? Down what road of danger were you about to travel? When you wake up, "if you do," what damage will have occurred? How many places will flesh be missing from the tongue, cheeks, and lips from being bit up? Will I have broken bones or just some knots on my head from crashing into something, you ask yourself. Thinking about these journeys are fearful. The duration of them and getting to the final destination of consciousness again is undetermined.

Absence seizures, (formerly Petit Mal) had mostly been replaced by the GTC seizures, (formerly Grand Mal) which would last for hours. I now experienced a condition called Status Epilepticus, seizures lasting more than five minutes. Many seizures following one after another fall under this definition. These types would often start with my left-hand closing. Over time, the hand would start closing tighter and tighter. Eventually, my arm would start to turn as if someone were grabbing and twisting it. The gripping would seem to let up momentarily, and then grip tighter. As the seizure intensified, it would throw me to the ground. Sometimes as the "brain" storm took control of my entire body, I would fall to the ground, still conscious. I experienced extreme pain from my body being contorted. After losing all control, I would then, go unconscious, waking up hours later. Status epilepticus is considered a medical emergency. I was surrounded completely by water, totally disconnected from emergency help. There were no phones or neighbors to elicit aid. Seizures so severe can cause brain swelling and possible injury or death. I would have many of these types of seizures. Prescribed by my doctor, my grandparents were given liquid phenobarbital to inject into my veins to bring me out of the repetitive seizures.

I recall one occasion where I regained consciousness after two days. Just before this, I had wanted to go fishing and break the monotony of the boring day. I had played all the war with spiders and bugs that I could stand for that day. I did not want to start working on the flower beds or the yard again. Nothing seemed to satisfy. I looked out and saw the new dock my grandfather and I had built. "Cootie, can I go fishing with my cane pole, Betsy?" She told me no, because I couldn't be watched and helped if a seizure were to happen. I remember getting upset with her and hollering,

"I'm sick and tired of being watched! I hate these seizures! I might as well be dead!" Feeling sorry for me and knowing I was just a boy wanting to have clean fun, Cootie relented. I went out on the dock with Betsy, my pole, in hand. All I wanted was to try and catch a fish. That couldn't be wrong, I reasoned with myself.

It was a bright, pretty day with a light breeze. I had been out there for such a short period of time enjoying myself when I suddenly felt that all too familiar feeling of an oncoming seizure. I remember looking at the shoreline about 40 feet away. I dropped Betsy and ran toward the shore. You know, I never saw that pole, my Betsy again.

That is what could have happened to me, falling into the water, never to be seen again. I only remember getting about halfway to shore. Cootie looked out the window of the small, two room house in which we were now living. I was nowhere to be seen.

As I reflect on this time in my life, filled with frustration and disappointment, it is crystal clear that Cootie, my grandmother, must have been a saint. I certainly had LOBBED PLENTY of my feelings onto her shoulders and she took them with grace. Indeed, I was loved.

Cootie And Me

Cootie tells the story, "I ran out of the house calling your name. I frantically looked around and then I began to cry. I thought you were gone, Johnny. I really did. Then I heard a gurgling sound over where the fishing net was hanging on the 2x4 nailed to the pine trees. There you lay, unconscious. I had brought a dish towel out with me unknowingly. I put it carefully in your mouth to keep you from biting your mouth so bad. I stayed out there in the sand with you until Uncle Bill finally came home. He injected you with phenobarbital, and it slowly brought you to the place where you had stopped seizing."

Uncle Bill noticed the imprint that the butt of the 2x4 had made across my collarbone. To him, it appeared broken since it jutted upward. They struggled and got me into the boat, and then into the car parked on the mainland. On the way to the hospital for X-rays, I began seizing again, one after another. Technicians at the hospital tried to take the X-rays between seizures. What an ordeal it was, Cootie said. She began talking to me hoping that hearing her voice would calm me. Eventually, they were able to take X- rays that showed my collarbone had been broken. They wrapped me and put padding around the entire bone. The seizure activity had slowed. Now, fully medicated, I would sleep the entire next day, while my brain recovered. As my collarbone mended, I was to hurt it several more times during subsequent seizures.

Shortly after this trying event, Cootie suffered her third heart attack. It was a severe one, and doctors said things did not look good for her. By God's mercy, she was to come home again to the island to heal and regain strength. I helped her all I could and continued to pray and read the Bible to her. Upon returning from this near-death heart attack, Cootie had declared to me, "*See, I came back, be-*

cause God knows my work is not finished until I get you raised. Not until we meet the woman who will replace me will I die." How do you know this?" I asked. "Grandmothers just know things, and God has promised me." I was to hear her say these words often in the coming years to really get me thinking. How could she be so sure of this, I wondered.

I enjoyed helping her get well by being there for her. If she needed me to dust, clean the kitchen, or scrub the floors, it was taken care of. I would help wash her hair and comb it out after drying it. When her toenails needed polished and her legs were needing a shave, I would carefully take care of them. Without suitable glasses, she was unable to shave her legs, fearful she might cut her varicose veins. Cootie trusted my eyes and my steady hand to use the razor to do this for her. "I sure don't want to take a chance of cutting myself around these big ugly' veins." She would also refer to the fact that she was on blood thinner. "I'm a bleeder, you know because I take rat poison." This is what she called her blood thinning medication.

Uncle Bill collected rainwater in 55-gallon drums, located below the front and the back of the sloped roof. This would ensure us usually having enough water to wash clothes in the old wringer washing machine. Being a typical boy, I would try to see how close I could place my fingers up to the rollers without getting them caught. It was like taking a dare. If you take enough dares, you eventually lose. Well, I lost a time or two, but blessedly this machine was equipped with a stop measure. I could hit the lever that would stop the rollers and release my fingers.

To finally bring electricity to our island, Uncle Bill hooked up an old Briggs and Stratton motor that had a pulley with the belt running over to a generator. This would charge up four large army batteries that my Uncle Bob, my cousin Steve's dad, had provided for us. When working, this provided some lighting in the house for us, as well as power to a small 12-inch television, for limited use of course. We could pick up the one local UHF channel that was between Fort Pierce and Vero Beach. One channel was better than none and so was a 12-inch television, considered small in those days.

I had gotten a portable, plastic record player that ran on flashlight batteries. It was blue and white, and how I enjoyed playing records. The music seemed to take away the sad moments I was experiencing at the time, caused by the circumstances. Despite prescribed medication, severe seizures would continue. I started having crying jags. I would sometimes get out the handgun Uncle Bill kept in a metal ammo box. Ashamedly, I would think about using it to escape my lot in life. There was always this question, *what would God say about this*? I would thankfully, put it away and go out under the Australian pine trees away from the house, and talk to God about things. I would ask Him why things had to be this way.

Dear God, why do I have to be sick like this? Why do I feel so abandoned sometimes, even by you, God? Why do I feel like I want to kill myself and end all this loneliness?" I continued in prayer. ***Dear God, this***

loneliness and sickness are more than I can stand. What purpose God, does my life have?

Under the pines, He would bring to my mind His Word. I had read it many times. "O ye of little faith!" Then I would also hear my grandmother say, God will never put more on you than you can bear. I could not find this in the Bible, so, I went searching. What His promise really says is, "God is faithful, and He will not let you be tempted beyond your ability, but with the temptation He will also provide the way of escape, that you may be able to endure it."[2] Believing that God's Word is always TRUTH, this trust would sustain me in critical hurtful moments. In tears, God's promises would bring me peace.

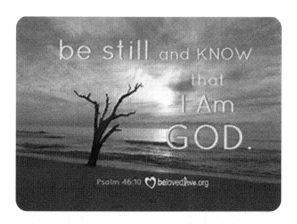

Somehow, I would always feel better after these heart-to-heart talks with God. I began spending much more time in prayer and even more time in His Word, asking and seeking answers.

The age of puberty brought many changes which threatened my young trust, a trust which had always uplifted me. What was happening to me? Could I hold on to God, or could God hold on to me? I was caught up into what seemed to be the recipe for a perfect destructive storm. A storm that brought health problems, loneliness, and struggles, seemingly with hurricane force gales, psychological outer bands that contributed to wave upon wave of epileptic seizures. In the middle of this would be the spawning of a tornado that threatened my foundation of belief, **But God!**

Being raised in South Florida, small changes in the weather were signs of what could be destructive happenings on the horizon. Stable weather usually existed when the winds blew from the east or southeast. In summer months, if these winds shifted to the southwest and west, temperatures, which were already warm, would get even hotter, often pushing into the high 90s. Storms would then spawn and sometimes wreak havoc. In winter months, one knew that colder than average temperatures were on the way with northwest winds. North to northeast winds in winter could represent a nor'easter, full of wind, cold, and rain, lasting sometimes for several days.

The years of being a tween (9-12) and on into puberty will show changes in all children, and like the weather, small differences usually bring larger challenging ones. With the onset of puberty, hormones bounce around like tiny atoms causing changes in the body that are heard, seen, and most disturbingly, felt. Even in the best of circumstances, these changes can be like shifting winds in the life of a young person during this tentative stage. Normal life changes can be challenging enough. When sickness, separation from society and close friends, and fear about a debilitating condition are thrown into the mix, what can be difficult is made more confusing. The years of growing can be breezy for some, stormy for others, and finally, a perfect cyclonic storm for those also bearing handicapping conditions.

Two Examples of Ignorance Rearing its Ugly Head

One barrier of many, for me, was how some people view certain disabilities. Their rude comments towards me aided the thoughts of not wanting to be on this earth. One protective mother, when finding out that her husband had allowed their child to visit the island while in his care was to say, "You let our child visit and walk around the island with a demon possessed boy? I forbid it." Ignorance can be hurtful, especially at this awkward age. Another such incident took place when my aunt took me home to Jacksonville, FL about 225 miles from the island. She was empathetic concerning my loneliness and being away from people. Upon arriving, she called her husband and told him she was home safe. She also said, "I brought Johnny home to stay awhile." Her husband went ballistic! and demanded that I be out of his home before he got there. She relented and had to take me back to the island. The round trip was about 450 miles. He was pugnacious and was willing to put his wife out that much to get rid of me. Sad! When hurtful things are said, remember to focus on that which is good, I said to myself. In that hurtful moment, I chose to take note of the kindness my aunt had shown me. I could not help but to remember Stacy's mom and her hateful comments a few months earlier. These types of verbal utterances stung and would bring sadness again and again. Satan would have me recall these words during my low points and *attempt to crush this clay that I am* at various times in the future. He fought to enslave me and to control my emotions, but heart to heart conversations with my Creator would stay him.

We may not wish to think about war, but I was to learn that there is spiritual warfare being waged against us every day. This war is waged for the capture of our souls. John Piper in "Don't Waste Your Life" writes about spiritual war being more deadly than an actual physical war. "In war time we ask different questions about what to do with our lives than we do in peace times. We ask: what can I do to advance the cause? What can I do to bring the victory? What sacrifice can I make or what risk can I take to insure the joy of triumph? In peacetime we ask, what can I do to be more comfortable? To have more fun. To avoid trouble and, possibly, avoid sin?"[3] In face-to-face combat, the soldier's body can be hurt or even killed. The visible enemy seeks to destroy our physical body. **In unseen spiritual warfare, Satan desires to raze our souls, made in the image of God.** God's Word weighs in on this topic saying,

"And do not fear those who kill the body but cannot kill the soul. Rather fear him who can destroy both soul and body in hell."[4] This should serve as a wakeup call to all who depend on traditions, good works, or even a church denomination to save us. In paraphrasing II Corinthians 12:15, Piper says, "A wartime lifestyle implies that there is a great and worthy cause for which to spend and be spent."[5] God was working His worthy cause in me.

Maturity brings the ability to ask questions and to explore the deeper meaning in what we read or have been taught. I began seeing what I viewed as discrepancies, not in God's Word, but in the teachings of my denomination, in which I had trusted. Since moving to the island, my grandparents had quit attending church. I began to rely on what I gleaned from personal Bible study. I could not always locate in scripture what I had been taught. I had loved God from my heart and did not want to lose connection with Him. What I could locate, again and again in the Bible, is that Jesus loved me. This deep-seated assurance would always bring me back from the brink of despair during my most difficult times of loneliness.

I remembered the words of a children's song, *"Jesus loves me, this I know, for the Bible tells me so."*

Maturity and discernment can also spawn complicated questions. Since Cootie and I spent most everyday working together in the flower garden, cleaning, walking, or just playing cards like Rummy and Solitaire, she was my 'go to' for answers about life.

Being around chihuahuas and chickens on the island was to teach me a lot about how puppies and chicks came to be. Cootie and Uncle Bill raised Chihuahuas to supplement their income. Each one had a name and was shown a lot of love. I had observed on many occasions, dogs mating and roosters getting down in the chicken yard. I knew that it took a male and a female for offspring. A female dog would become pregnant at certain times and a hen would sit on her eggs after making a nest. Having no conversations with other boys about these things, I observed nature. I also searched the Bible to see what God's Word had to say on these types of questions. It had much to say on the subject. I reviewed that God created male and female, and their differences are to be held in high respect. With all the visual aids from nature, I was sure I understood the concept, but how would it fit into my world?

When I spoke with Cootie about this new awareness, she was to give me a no holds barred answer packaged in simplicity. She used plumbing, a concept I could visualize. She said, "Well Johnny, you know that God equipped males and females with different fittings which come in various threading and sizes. In later years I was to learn that what she was referring to was concave and convex. Concave fittings are female and convex fittings are male. She said that the wonderful way God had made people is that even though each is equipped with different sizes, both adjust to one another in lovemaking when the two connect their private parts together. She went on to say that the male part inserted and dispensed the male seed that would fertilize the female egg causing a baby to be formed. She explained to me that the residue I was concerned about, which I had seen from time to time, was called sperm. She said this carried the male seed. I knew about seeds and how they worked when planted in the garden. When planted, the seeds would sprout new flowers. "You mean I have the ability to make a baby?" "Yes," she continued, "The sad thing about people is that they all too often cannot be satisfied with their mate. People are always wondering if a different size fitting would be even better than what they already have. This is all in their heads, because if they tried another size, they would become tired of it and continue their quest for the perfect connection. Johnny, Honey, there are no perfect connections. The connections God has given you, will become perfect between you and the one you love. Whatever plumbing you have, basically operates the same, when you get right down to it. Cherish the one God brings into your life. He will also show you that the physical will always be superseded by what is in your heart. Trust God, Honey, for that right person." I responded, "But Cootie, who is going to be my girlfriend and learn to love me? I am not around anyone." Her answer was as always, "You will need to trust me on this. God has someone special just for you." We ended our conversation with Cootie suggesting, "Let's step away from this serious talk and play a few hands of Rummy. I will bet you a nickel that I can beat you." *"You're on,"* I replied.

Chapter Ten Endnotes

1. *John 8:44c*

2. *I Corinthians 10:13b*

3. *John Piper, Don't Waste Your Life. (Wheaton: Crossway, 2009) 111- 112,118*

4. *Matt. 10:28*

5. *John Piper, Don't Waste Your Life. 113-114*

Chapter Eleven

CHERISHED MEMORIES

While isolated, island life still handed me some cherished times. It would afford me the time needed to study and read. I enjoyed American and World History, along with Science and Geography of all types. Language was also fascinating with all its grammar rules. I spent many hours just reading words in the dictionary and learning their meanings. Math was sometimes boring, I must confess, but when I would conquer an equation or word problem, I felt the excitement of conquering Goliath.

Reading scripture brought me God's Word that promised His love for me. Reading and studying would bring satisfaction. It would transport me around the world, even if only in my mind. Yes, I was traveling the globe, all with the use of books. If only laptops and desktops had existed, no worries, if they had existed, I didn't have the means to recharge their batteries!

I remember the night sitting with Uncle Bill and Cootie, often on the end of the dock over the water. The night skies were beautiful with stars galore. Every now and then one would be moving. Uncle Bill explained to me that I was watching a satellite. The beautiful full moons were sensational as they popped up on the eastern horizon. Fish would be jumping around in the water making a delightful splashing sound, mixed with the water itself ever so gently making a rippling sound along the shoreline. I felt so loved, being there with both of my grandparents and chatting a little about a lot of different subjects. Sometimes if the phosphorus levels were high, caused by water runoff from the mainland, one could see the fish trail left behind. It would appear as a white flash as the fish went by. We could have two low tides and two high tides within a 24-hour times span. The Saint Lucie inlet worked as a commode removing pollution from the lagoon, preventing bacteria buildup. The water in it rushed out toward the sea during low tides and brought back into the lagoon freshwater from the Atlantic during high tides in the intracoastal.

West Dock and Fishing Barge

An exciting time for me was fishing off the floating barge Uncle Bill had built. He would anchor it just outside the main channel of the Indian River lagoon. With a lantern hanging over the water, one could see to scoop up shrimp three to four inches in length. Blue Crabs could also be trapped in a crab trap that had been baited with cut up fish. All of this was going on while you were waiting for a fish to take your bait on the hook of your trusted cane pole. Being next to the channel, one never knew what size fish would take your bait and run with your line, making it sing. Under watchful eyes, pushing up shrimp from the grass around the shoreline was also fun. Uncle Bill had taught me to slide my feet along the bottom when in the water. Stingrays would bury themselves into the sand, thus sliding your feet allowed you to bump them instead of stepping on them. Stepping on one would allow them to break off their barbs into your foot; strictly self-defense. Barbs were jaded, so going in was easy, but coming out would rip the flesh. Sometimes the need to cut them out became a reality. The stingray's barb is covered in a mildly **venomous** sheath of skin. When the barb is pushed into a foreign body, the venom is dispersed. The venom consists of a protein-based toxin that causes a lot of pain in and around the area and may also **alter the heart rate and respiration of the victim.** For senior citizens who visit the area and have wading and fishing in Florida as part of their itinerary, avoiding the barb of the stingray could be important, especially if you already have issues with your heart. Being an island boy, I was to learn about the dangers of the barb of the ray from Uncle Bill. His knowledge in the 60s is on par with data known in 2021.

Another joy that I cherished, after several years of being on the island, was being rejoined with my sister Rose Marie. We had not lived together with our grandparents since she was seven and I was nine, now we were both teenagers. Back then she dressed up, teased her hair, and held a pretend cigarette intending to imitate Comedian Phyllis Diller. She often quoted one of Diller's jokes, "I'm so old, my elbows leak!" And then another, "Oh, Darling, Fang just loves this dress!" Rose Marie would hold up a tutu.

As I explained in Chapter 7, Rose Marie's concern for me was a fond memory, along with how she would turn to me to share things about how much Jesus loves her and me. Besides trying to understand me and the many hardships of my epilepsy, she would always try to protect and defend me when I was made fun of. One such defense took place when I was ten and she was eight. I had tried to live with my mother for a while and things did not go well. Her husband was an alcoholic. He could be nice when sober and quite mean and nasty when drinking. He and I clashed because I would tell him how the Bible says that all drunkards were going to hell, and that he was going to burn in hell for being a drunk. At 10, I was a literalist and could tend to sometimes hit people with God's Word, instead of in love sharing His Word with them.

Today, I am still one who believes in the literal Word of God, however, with maturity and growth in the Lord, came the awareness that we are to share God's Word in love and not as a sledgehammer. Scripture teaches that we do not change people. Our job is to sow and water.

The Holy Spirit woos the sinner to Christ.

"Go tell," said the Angel to Jesus' followers when they watched him ascend into the heavens. The promise given to them was that this same Jesus will come in like manner. We can apply this promise and all of God's Word to our own lives *literally.*

The way I delivered God's Word hit a sore spot with my mom's husband, and he began hitting on me, my sister to the rescue yet again! Rose Marie went and put on a white pointed dress shoe, and while he hit me, she kicked him between the legs and yelled, "Run Johnny, run!" He went down and I ran.

Now that she was coming to be with us awhile, maybe she could help me tie boats to docks. A simple half hitch would do. She taught me how to tie my shoes when I was in the third grade. I was blessed that she was on her way.

Rose Marie would attend school while with us. Uncle BILL would take her by boat to the mainland. They then would transfer to the vehicle, and Marie would be dropped off at the bus stop on Torpy Rd. and US 1.

I remember thinking how nice it must have been to go to school and to be with your friends. Marie met a girl named Joanne at the bus stop and they became friends. Friends! what a treasure they are to us when we bond together. Most certainly, when friends are there to lift each other up, it is pleasing to God. Jesus calls those who believe in Him, friends, *if they do what He commands.*[1] Over the years I have learned a valuable lesson, new friends are like silver, and long-lasting ones are like gold; their value always increases. But if Jesus is our friend, *what does He command us to do?* Island Boy would ponder this question, along with others, and would discover what Jesus truly meant to be a true friend of His. After all, even Satan believes in Jesus, and he certainly is not a friend to God's Son.

This memoir is being written during the coronavirus COVID-19 of 2020 and 2021. This plight upon humanity has been costly in untold ways. Many people today are ripped from their friends. Some are isolated in hospitals, nursing homes, and from their jobs. Children have been kept from school and friends, some much longer than others. The largest groups affected have been the elderly and children. Consider how many seniors have spent their final days alone, cut off from the world. The emotional toll, increased anxiety and isolation is prevalent. Recent research indicates a spike in suicides of anywhere between 15% in seniors and as high as a 67% increase in some areas of the country for teens committing suicide.[2] Speaking from personal experience, isolation is a hard road to travel at any age, and some are at a greater risk. I have such empathy for those who are isolated and finding their lives turned upside down, inside out. My barriers were water and seizures, separating me from society. The common thread in all of this is the desire to get well, stay well, and to rejoin fellowship with others. I also wanted to regain some sense of fitting in. My own discontinuity at this time, where I left the normal and entered the abnormal, caused by illness, separation from school and friends, was to last for many years. I know ONLY God kept me. Isolation had taken me down a path of hopelessness, as it has many during this pandemic. If just one could know all God has in store for them during these valleys! I wish that I could teach everyone to reach out to God and pray at a young age and sow seeds of trust in the God who has made them. For He has promised never to desert us, to always be with us, forever and ever. The COVID-19 pandemic has exposed a need in society to have a trust in the designer, Almighty God. When human foundations are shaken, the architect must be consulted, as one would consult the architect of a building with structural weakness.

Chapter Eleven Endnotes

1. John 15:14
2. www.thedoctorstv.com/articles/the-teen...

Chapter Twelve

REMEMBRANCES OF LOVE, TRUST, AND DELIVERANCE

I was taught to pray at a young age as described in chapter one, and a trust blossomed between me and my maker. Yes, childlike trust/faith that God knows all, and cares is important at any age. One is never too old for this trust to begin. The benefits are immeasurable, and the sooner the better. I can attest that early trust in the architect kept me from doing myself harm when I was at my lowest emotional ebb as a teenager. I am so appreciative that my grandmother taught me how to pray. I am much older now, than in the 1960s, but I can testify the words of Ecclesiastes, chapter 3, verse 15 which says, **"Whatever is, has already been, and whatever will be, already is."**

The American Heritage Dictionary shows that trust and faith are synonyms. In the rules of grammar, we learn that a synonym is a word that has the same meaning or nearly the same. When a person learns to pray to their creator

God, they do so in trust. When you learn someone is good, in trust you will desire to talk and share with them your heart's concerns. **"Taste and see that the Lord is good. How happy is the man who takes refuge in Him!"**[1]

In life's twists and turns, we need to take refuge in the one who has made us. Like with any architect, a creator must be trusted that what they have created will withstand. If God created me in love, and pure love is perfect, then it stands to reason that He will make a way, but how? Because I was taught to pray and trust in the architect of the world, I began testing and tasting the goodness of God. He was to show me just how much He loved me. He would take care of not only the needs that were seen, but those that were unseen. Oh! But the clay that I am had to be dragged along for the journey; then, and sometimes even today. The Bible reminds us that indeed the spirit is willing, but the flesh is weak.[2]

For now, Rose Marie was here with me. She loved me and I knew it. What a joy it was to have someone close to my age to talk with and to enjoy. She was just enough of a tomboy for this boy to appreciate. Because of her being with me I could go fishing more. Together we would also busy ourselves looking for dinosaur bones and teeth. She played songs on the radio and danced to them, something she and Cootie had in common. Although a grandmother, Cootie had enjoyed dancing all her life as mentioned in chapter 5. In fact, she would tell us when she was young, she and Uncle Bill could sure cut the rug (referring to dancing) She said that people would clear the dance floor and watch them dance at times. I guess you could have called them the Fred Astaire and Ginger Rogers of their town.

Yes, Rose Marie brought me a needed friend, herself. I even got to drive in the boat with her at my side. Such relief, how refreshing! Only God could do this for me. I was saddened when Marie went back to Georgia to live. Our mother had lived there since I was nine years old. She had made this move to Green County, GA where her father's family still resided. I suppose it gave her comfort to be near her father's people.

Her dad's brother, Virgil Moon, operated a small gas station/grocery store in Greensboro called Moon's Grocery. He was married to a sweet woman named Grace. His sister Ruth was also dear. I had been told over the years by my grandmother about Robert Ceals Moon. He was my mother's biological father. He died as a young man after having a tooth extracted. Infection set in and went quickly to sepsis. In 1938, sepsis was almost a sure death sentence. My mother was only three when her father died during the years of the Great Depression.

It started on a Friday, in 1929, which became known as Black Friday, with the collapse of the stock market. It was to officially last until 1938, but it would be America entering World War II on December 7, 1941, that would eventually spawn a booming economy. America would emerge as the only superpower in the world and victor over Germany and Japan. Depression and war were tough and difficult times, But God... God was to win over evil.

Because of the suffering of the Jewish people in the Holocaust during the Nazi reign in Germany and in most of Europe, many Jews would desire to turn back to their homeland. They would echo the cries of their ancestors after being kept in Egypt for four hundred plus years. Many of these years were spent as slaves to the Egyptians with much suffering. In 1446 BC, God would deliver them out of the bondage and suffering.

Again, in history, by 1948, the Jewish people had reestablished a Jewish state, which had not existed since 70 AD. They had been kept as slaves and many millions had died under Adolph Hitler and his Nazi party; started in 1933. By 1939, this murderous party had not only begun to try to rule the world, but also to exterminate the Jewish race just as Haman had tried to do, as recorded in the book of Esther. But God... Haman was defeated by the hand of God. God caused miraculous events to take place using the right people at the right time to stop the extermination of the Jewish people, from whom Jesus Christ would descend.

According to the book of Esther, Mordecai's young Jewish cousin, Hadassa, (Esther) had blossomed into a beautiful lady who had been taken in by a decree of King Ahasuerus of the Persian Empire. Through a series of events, all right on time as God would deem it, Esther would become

Ahasuerus' queen. When the Jews were threatened, God had this Jewish young lady in place. Mordecai asked for her help in stopping this murderous plan that Haman had orchestrated. He was to tell her, "For if you keep silent at this time, relief and deliverance will rise for the Jews from another place, but you and your father's house will perish. And who knows whether you have not come to the kingdom for such a time as this?"[3]

Mordecai had learned to trust God at an early age. With maturity, guided by the Holy Spirit, an amazing process takes place. Trust is something which must be earned. A missionary will gain trust by providing food, shelter, and medical supplies. Once physical trust has been established, the missionary will then move to address the most important need that anyone has, the spiritual. Your children trust you because they know you desire only their best. An animal, such as a dog, trusts you as it greets you with its wagging tail. The difference in the child's trust and the pet's trust is that the dog's trust will never present itself as faith. Only humans created in God's image can know faith. It is our Creator who plants the seed of trust. When it germinates and matures, as it can only within the soul given to mankind, it can then develop into faith. God starts with showing us that He can be trusted in all ways. The Holy Spirit nourishes this trust in us. When we, through the Holy Spirit recognize what Christ has done for us through the shedding of His uniquely perfect blood for our sins, we are drawn by the Holy Spirit in faith to accept Christ as Lord and Savior.

The Covid 19 pandemic reminds us of society's greatest need, God.

"...Men always ought to pray, and not lose heart."[4] The architect who created us desires to hear from us. Have you talked to your Creator today? If you have not, He is waiting for you. Tell Him about things. He will hear your voice. Ask yourself, what special mission has God called me to in His Kingdom? Island Boy will testify how the seed of trust grew into faith in chapter fourteen.

Chapter Twelve Endnotes

1. *Psalm 34:8*
2. *Matthew 26:41b*
3. *Esther 4:14*
4. *Luke 18:1{NKJV}*

Chapter Thirteen

BELIEVE IT OR NOT!

If you are reading this chapter, you know that it is number 13. Many people fear this number. It has a psychological name called Triskaidekaphobia. (triski deka fobea) This term comes from two Greek words, triskaideka meaning thirteen and QoBos (fobos) meaning fear, dread, and terror. From QoBos evolves our English word phobia. A fear or phobia can be based on a real-life event or perhaps a superstition passed down from many centuries of a supposed odd happening.[1] Omission of the number 13 can be found in many places. Cruise ships will often skip the 13th deck and go to 14. Buildings, hotels, and elevators will often avoid #13, due to Triskaidekaphobia. It is estimated that millions of dollars are lost every Friday the 13th, because people avoid flying, driving, and shopping. Interesting enough, fear of the combination Friday and thirteen is called paraskevidekatriaphobia.[2] Among various websites, information may be found concerning this subject, such as Wikipedia and elsewhere listed in the footnotes.

> **Fret Not Yourself;**
> **It Tends Only to Evil.**
> Psalm 37:8b

Island Boy had many things to fret and dread. But God... Yes, God had revealed himself as one who could be trusted. Little did I realize that a transformational event was looming in the not-too-distant future, an encounter that would change my life forever. I had become a boy who feared little due to life circumstances, and because of a God in whom I trusted. I was raised in severe poverty, but I didn't realize it because I felt loved by my Creator and grandparents. We see in I John 4:18 these words, "There is no fear in love, but perfect love casts out all fear." The second part of this verse says that fear has to do with punishment. When we have fears or phobia, real or imaginary, we are not trusting in the love of God. It may be hard for us to keep from fretting, to set aside our fears and phobias. John Ortberg, in his book, *If You Want to Walk on Water, You've Got to Get Out of the Boat,* reminds us, "The single command in Scripture that occurs more often than any other- God's most frequent repeat instruction- is formulated in these words, FEAR NOT..." He goes on to say, "I think God says 'Fear Not' so often because fear is the number one reason human beings are tempted to avoid doing what God asks them to do. Fear is the number one reason human beings are tempted to avoid getting out of the boat."[3] My boat was an island setting, with water all around, still cut off from society and friends. I had to trust God that He would not let me sink in despair.

I was to step out of my island boat several times over the years, convinced that everything would be OK. I was believing that God would grant me some relief from seizures. With this trust and hope securely in my mind, I journeyed to Union Point, Georgia, from the island in South Florida. I knew I was stepping into rough waters in going there in the first place. As I described in Chapter 11, my mother's husband and I did not get along due to his drinking and my condemnation of his overindulgence in alcohol. I was 15 years of age, and Cootie had been in touch with my mother, saying that she feared I might die in some of my seizure episodes. She could not continue to watch me seize for hours. My mother called a hospital in Augusta, GA. They agreed to admit me and observe to see if anything could be done to help. It would be a month or so before they could transport me to Greene County Georgia, where my mother had lived now for many years.

By this time, Uncle Bill had built a third room onto our two-room house which gave me a bedroom. We had come a long way from the beginning where we slept in a tent for many months. Next I slept on a cot at the foot of my grandparents' bed, and now I have a room of my own. "Wow!" I thought.

One morning waking up, I was laying there listening to the sounds of the birds and the chickens. Suddenly, I saw Jesus sitting on a throne. He was surrounded with what appeared to be Cherubim. I was frozen in place for a moment. As I gazed up to the ceiling where this was originating, I heard Jesus say, "Come!" Immediately everything ended. I could once again move, and I quickly put on my everyday shorts and sought Cootie to tell what had just happened. She cried. She was afraid this was a sign that I would be taken during a seizure. She recalled one of the many times she was putting holy water on me and asking God to please let me live. She had a strong thought, almost voice like in her head, "Don't worry about Johnny, he belongs to me." These two events were almost not retold in this memoir, but as a missionary friend told me, "God works in unusual ways when circumstances are dire." He had witnessed the impossible occur when needed. Our lives were under unusual and difficult hardships. God transcends all. Even in seemingly impossible situations, God is still God.

A few weeks later my mother arrived to take me home with her. She had brought my brothers and sisters with her. It was so nice seeing everyone and it felt good to hug each other. I kept the biggest hug for my mom. Another strange thing was about to happen. The next day the oldest of my siblings and I, went around to the north side of the island to wade out and fish. We had pushed up our shrimp in the cove for bait and made our way with poles in hand. We caught several jacks, drum fish, and some snapper. If memory serves me right, Marie caught one of her favorites, grouper. On our way back to the southside of the island, we were anxious to show our catch off, when something happened. I have no memory of this, except I know I woke up an hour or two later. My siblings were mortified by what they witnessed. They said, as we were returning, I dropped my fishing pole and started walking into the water. As they watched me get waist deep, they were screaming, "Johnny, come back! what are you doing?" If I had not been told these details, I wouldn't know a thing, for as I said, I had no memory of the incident. They explained that I responded with this, "Don't you see them?" They replied, "See what?" I said, "The snakes, dancing on top of the water. They are calling me to come to them." By this time, the water had gotten up to my shoulders and Rose Marie led the way, they said, as they all came out to help drag me back to shore.

In retrospect, there seemed to have been a spiritual battle going on for my life and soul, in these difficult early teen years. Truth is, there is a spiritual battle for each of our lives and souls. Sometimes the battle is more pronounced, even visible, depending on our circumstances. Ephesians 6:12-13 describes this war. "For we do not wrestle against flesh and blood, but against the rulers, against the authorities, against the cosmic powers over this present darkness, against the spiritual forces of evil in the heavenly places. Therefore, take on the whole armor of God, that you may be able to withstand..." In modern society, one is seen as a nut job if the spiritual battle is acknowledged.

Scripture records that Satan embodied a serpent who carried on a conversation with Eve.[4] Additionally, Satan and his cohorts tried to enslave the people of Corinth. In this setting we see Satan appearing as an Angel of

"Did God actually say, 'You shall not eat of any tree in the garden'?" Gen. 3:1

light and deceitful workmen disguising themselves as apostles of Christ.[5]

Paradoxical to Satan, The Holy Spirit is a person who genuinely cares for you and me. He is the third person of the Trinity. The Spirit of God can appear or manifest himself in bodily form, a figure or other outward appearance. This third person of the Trinity can take the form of wind, breath, and spirit. The Hebrew word *ruach* and the synonym *pneuma,* from the Greek are used to indicate this phenomenon. The Spirit brings about God's awesome power on display, or his gentle quietness and peace. An entire book and much more could be written on the third person of the Godhead. The Holy Spirit has been seen as a dove,[6] tongues of fire,[7] the one who dried up the Red Sea or Reeds.[8] He is also known as the Comforter, whom Jesus sent after He physically left His apostles and believers.[9] The Holy Spirit now resides in every Christian, empowering us to live free and accomplish much for the Father in Heaven.[10]

Upon returning to Georgia with mom and family, I waited another few weeks before the hospital in Augusta could admit me. I remember our ride from Union Point to Augusta vividly. My mother and her husband took me there. Larry had to have a few cans of his favorite beer for the trip, Pabst Blue Ribbon. As we drove, a severe thunder and lightning storm occurred. It rained heavily. About one hour into the trip, my mother saw in the woods, young men jogging through the red mud of Georgia, in military attire, with their backpacks. They were on a training exercise at

Fort Gordon's Army Base. My mother shed some tears because of what they were having to do in this bad storm, rain, and mud. She said, "I feel so sorry for those boys." Larry went off. "Shut up before I push you out there with them," he hollered. Silence in the car...I sat in the back seat wondering why a couple beers changed his whole personality. He could really get angry fast after drinking just a little. This was sad, because he could also be helpful and nice, minus the alcohol. He was intelligent and could superbly play those ebony and ivory keys of the piano. In fact, years earlier, he and his brothers had a group called the Paschal Rascals. What a shame for such talent to be sunk by an intoxicating liquid. Sitting in the backseat not saying a word, I remembered Rose Marie telling how he would also drink bottles of Nervine, a then over the counter nerve liquid. One day at her disgust, she came home from school and found Larry naked inside the gas kitchen oven with bottles of Nervine scattered around on the floor. He was trying to get warm but could not reach the knob that supplied the spark to the pilot light which would ignite the oven. My sister, in keeping with her personality said, "I should have assisted him." Rose gave off one of her Phillis Diller laughs. Can you picture this scene? Larry was smart and gifted but wasted so much due to addiction. Again, this is what Satan does. He seeks to destroy the gifts given to us by God, and will embody anyone, thing, or substance if allowed.

We made it to the state-run Medical College of Georgia. It was named after Eugene Talmage, who had been a governor of the Peach state, serving three terms in office before his death in 1946.[11] I would stay there several weeks and was assigned a team of doctors who would observe my health. A member of that group would be a psychiatrist. (I wondered why.) I later learned, there were some epileptics, who could throw themselves into seizures. Wow! That certainly was not me. I had prayed that God would take this thorn in the flesh from me. They could never seem to find anything to help me. I was a puzzle to them. My electroencephalogram, "EEG" recorded such erratic brain waves. Looking on the bright side, it wasn't flatlined. Doctors concluded, yes, I suffered from epilepsy. The scarred brain tissue was apparent, and the severity of the seizures could be exacerbated by puberty. Little information could be given, but something sinister would soon take place.

My desire to honor God was placed on trial and I didn't even know it. I would later become aware, that as a patient, all of my activities while at Talmadge were being logged and given to the psychiatrist. who had been told by my mom's husband Larry that I was a religious fanatic. I have written in an earlier chapter about praying to God. Praying daily, and often had become part of my life. Every night, even in the hospital, I would kneel beside my steel bed and pray. During the day, I was taken to the art and craft activity room. I was given several different options to create. I chose to make an angel. I received a stencil to copy onto plywood. I then glued string for the outline. Finally, I glued colorful crusted pebbles to fill in the design. It turned out beautifully, and I kept it for many years.

The psychiatrist often probed me with questions. One such inquiry, as I look back, is quite telling. *It has been said that Satan is a sly old fox, if I could catch him, I'd put him in a box.*

Lucifer, aka Satan/ Devil runs free, to and fro among us.
Job 1:7

He asked me in one of the sessions, "What would you do if a girl leaned over and you could see her panties, or saw that she had none on at all?" I replied, "Well, I would turn my head and look elsewhere." To which he replied, "John, that is an unusual answer for a teenage boy. Most boys would want to see more. Why would you turn your head and not want to see more," he asked? With assurance, I answered, "Because Jesus would have me do this. He would not be pleased with me staring at a girl's private area."

Over our many sessions together, I remember telling him openly and innocently about my many prayers on the island and how God had shown me that He could be trusted. In fact, I was to tell him about a joyous occasion that God had brought about just a week or so before coming to the hospital. Satan is the prince of the air and at work in the sons of disobedience.[12] Unsuspecting me, I could not have imagined what evil loomed next.

A few days before I was to leave the hospital, Cootie had been brought to Union Point. She had a sore so severe that it would not heal. Mom had talked to a local physician, Dr Rhodes, about her condition and that she had little money to have anything done about it. He said, "Mary if you can get her here to Georgia, I will look into what I can do." Upon examining her, he removed the sore surgically. It was tested by the labs and was found to be benign. Cootie healed quickly and we were all thankful. God's timing had brought Cootie to Union Point at a critical time for me. My mother had been advised that the psychiatrist felt I could benefit from a hospital in Milledgeville. Larry quickly convinced my mother that this would be a good thing. After all, the hospital 's name includes the word Epileptics. "Seeking more help for John couldn't be a bad thing," Larry added. My mother conceded, "I suppose not," she reportedly said. Little did she know that Larry had been talking to the psychiatrist about long term institutionalization for me. My mom had no real understanding what this hospital was, and therefore signed off without further information. The psychiatrist said he would arrange for me to be transferred in the coming days.

When I was discharged from the hospital in Augusta, I went to my mom's home overnight. Cootie was waiting for my return there. It was so good to see her, and she told me all about Doctor Rhodes and what a caring, nice person he was. We talked late and got up early to set out for Milledgeville the next morning with my mom and Rose Marie. Upon arrival, mom showed papers to the guard at the entrance. A concrete wall and gate surrounded it. Upon entering, we all recognized that this was not a regular hospital. Rose Marie pointed to the short stout man pretending to direct traffic. He had a toy gun, whistle, and dressed in khaki pants with a plastic badge on his shirt. Rose Marie said,

"Momma, that man acts touched in the head." She quietly laughed as he tried to stop and move traffic. The man pointed in all directions, blowing hard on the whistle. Mom continued to drive, following the posted directions. Cootie said, "That man just isn't right." Rose Marie thoroughly resisted this place. We arrived at the building where all four of us got out of the car. Inside, Mom presented an office clerk her paperwork. At a certain point, just inside this old gray building, my family was stopped and told they could go no further. I was taken up a steep flight of metal stairs with a big heavy door at the top. A big, strong looking man opened the door with a key. On the other side, another world was waiting for me. My mother, grandmother, and sister all went back to the person to whom they had given their paperwork. Almost simultaneously, mom and Cootie asked, "What is this place?" The office clerk answered, *"The Georgia State Mental and Epileptic Asylum."* Fear struck my family, as there had to be a huge mistake made, and my mother demanded to have me back. She went and talked to someone in charge who explained that without checking with the admitting doctor and proving the mistake, that I could not be released. My mother demanded something be done. She was told that it would take a while to contact the proper people. They advised my family to leave, and maybe the following day something could take place, as it was already getting close to noon.

To give a little history of this institution, the asylum was opened in 1842, and has operated in some form continuously since accepting its first patient. It was founded as the **Georgia State Lunatic, Idiot, and** (Get this!) **Epileptic Asylum**. It has also been called the Georgia State Sanitorium and Milledgeville State Hospital during its long history. By the 1960's, when I was admitted, the facility had grown to the largest mental hospital in the world, contending with Pilgrim Psychiatric Center in New York. The asylum in Milledgeville once boasted of two hundred buildings on two-thousand acres housing over 12,000 patients.[13] You read it right! Epileptics were strewn throughout that number. Epileptics have had much to overcome due to society's fear and the categorizing of their condition. In the 1960s, epileptics were still being hidden. Society continued to be influenced by generations of false tales and phobias, while living under the shroud of darkness, fueled by ignorance regarding the nature of epilepsy.

I personally credit Martin Luther King's leadership in breaking down the barriers between races in our country as being pivotal for all people to be included, even the handicapped. He said he dreamed of a day when a person will be judged by the content of his character instead of the color of his skin. The epileptic and many others have had much ignorance and a stigma attached to their handicapping conditions. They could rightly cry out, "Judge me by character and not by my condition..." History shows that barriers began to wane with King's words, "I Have a Dream" The consciousness of the civil rights of all people was being strengthened and enlightened.

My family returned home, and Larry met them in the large kitchen. He had been drinking. Cootie said that my mom had surely shown her love for me that day. Besides fighting for my release at the now recognized asylum, she would also face off with Larry. Larry reportedly said, "Well, I've done it now, I've gotten rid of your religious fanatic son, with the help of that psychiatrist. I told him your son was a sick fanatic in his belief in God and he agreed by what he had observed and logged in his notes." Cootie was to tell me, "Your mother flew into him, clawing his face with her nails. Blood came streaming down Larry's cheeks. She jumped on his back, clawing him, and knocking him to the ground. He pushed her away and got up and ran out the door, as your mother threw a pot at him." Cootie added, "There was no doubt how much your mother loves you! A loving mother will fight fearlessly for her kids. Today, she sure fought for you like a Mama Bear."

Meanwhile, there I stood, in a large dank grey room with a myriad of things happening before my eyes. I had no idea what mom was doing to secure my release. She later explained that the word Epileptics was in the name of the institution and thus it was sold to her as a place where she could get help for me. Larry's intentions were kept from her. The large room had dozens of people acting strange and bizarre. **"Dear God," I thought. "I am in the crazy house! How has this happened?"** I prayed and asked God to rescue me, to calm my fears. *Jesus loves me this I know for the Bible tells me so.* I would hold on to these words. He had always shown how much he loved me through his actions on my behalf, especially in what he had done for me a few weeks before entering Talmage Hospital in

Augusta. *God, I know you are going to provide a way for me.* I stopped and prayed for the poor souls roaming around making all kinds of odd noises, bumping into one another. Many were sleeping on the floor, yet others came over trying to communicate and touch me. Most all seemed sedated in one way or another. The night would be long, and every now and then the Strong Man would open the steel door and look in. Keep in mind, this was in the day before cameras monitored most locations. I thought, I have got to get out of this place, but how? I noticed a small mat on the floor in front of the steel door with no windows. I would spend a big part of the night using that mat trying to escape. The idea was to run over to the door and try to get the mat pushed between the door and the jamb just enough to keep it from locking. I also thought, what if it did stop the door from closing all the way and the Strong Man would notice and return when he did not hear the clunk of the door as he walked down the stairs. He most certainly would come and investigate, I reasoned. I questioned myself, what to do if he comes back? Where there's a will, there's a way, I schemed. On each attempt to catch the door, I would run back to the population and fall to the floor to pretend I was asleep. On other occasions I would run and jump back into the population where others were milling around from place to place making groans.

The stench was horrendous, as you can imagine, with so many people not bathed and using the bathroom on self or otherwise. All night I had prayed and stayed alert, on guard, and had made it to what I called the fourth watch,

3 am – 6 am. Beginning when Israel was conquered by the Romans, the Jews had taken on a fourth watch instead of just three watches. The Intertestamental period had been about four hundred years and many changes had taken place in Israel with foreign occupation. The Greek and Roman military had divided the night into four watches to guard the night hours more safely.

Being in this abyss on earth gives one a glimpse of Hell, minus the fire, with souls knocking into each other, groaning, and tormented in their existence. I had read Dante's Inferno with its different levels of torment in Hell. What level was I on? Dante's Inferno is fictional, based in part on truth found in God's Word, the Holy Scriptures, which are inerrant and infallible.[14] I again comforted myself with God's truth. "I am with you always..."[15]

God is our refuge and strength, a very present help in trouble. Therefore, we will not fear though the earth gives way, though the mountains be moved into the heart of the sea, though its waters roar and foam, though the mountains tremble at its swelling. There is a river whose streams make glad the city of God, the holy habitation of the Most High. God is in the midst of her; she shall not be moved; God will help her when morning dawns.
Psalms 46:1- 4

Yes, doing this military, staying alert maneuver, in such a dangerous and odious place, I was able to make the mat catch the door. It did not lock as the Strong Man made his way down the stairs. Would he notice the absence of the locking sound? I waited to see while faking sleep on the floor with the others. The door opened wide and Strong Man stood in the opening. He shouted with a nasty growl, "Which one of you idiots are playing games? Leave the (expletive) door alone or you will be punished!" I had tried throughout the night many times, and each time I would blend among the dozens around me, getting much practice, just in case the door did not catch, and he would notice. "Shew!" I was glad I was not caught.

Morning would soon arrive, and I could only hope and pray that Mama and Cootie were working hard to correct this dismal situation. Remember I said that I was in Georgia at the beginning of this chapter a few weeks before Talmadge and now the sanitarium in Milledgeville? I had come there, as you read, to get help with my epilepsy, **But God!** *God had other plans for me and my life before these hospital stays had ever taken place.*

Around 10:00 am, the following day, I was taken from the large grey room, with its fullness of misery, and brought down the stairs to a small one. I waited a few minutes there and my Cootie and Mama came through the doors. We hugged each other and joyously cried. A nightmare had come to an end. Mom had successfully proven to them that she had not known that Larry had collaborated with the psychiatrist to put me here long term. Larry was, as I mentioned, a smart man. He could also be very persuasive. He had been tapped by the United States Army, along with a handful of others recognized for their brilliance. This group was to come up with a plan which would neutralize Rommel, the tank commander in World War Two, known as the Desert Fox.

Later in life I would learn that Sigmund Freud, a biologist, physiologist and later known as the father of psychoanalysis, would pioneer what most psychiatrists and psychologists would come to believe, for many decades, concerning the function of the human mind. He also wanted to be known as the father of Modern-Day Psychology, but there were also five other professionals who considered themselves to be the Father of Psychology.[16] He would have no trouble claiming this title for himself, since the "ID," which Freud called the **pleasure principle** aimed to ensure that it is granted the pleasure it seeks. He was not a neurologist by training, nonetheless, he would claim to be a professional in neurology.[17]

Another Freudian claim is found in his book, Moses and Monotheism. Here we find Freud trying to be a scholar in Old Testament works concerning Moses. He attempts to debunk the Biblical account of Moses' birth to Jochebed. As in most of Freud's areas of endeavor, he was faux; yes, an imposter. According to many, such as Aliant International University, much of what Freud taught has been proven to be wrong and is an outdated fossil. Some of what he taught could even be dangerous to the general public. In my opinion, his teaching of "penis envy" stands right up there with the fallacy of his writings about Moses in the Bible. You may ask, "What is this envy?" According to Freud, penis envy is a stage of development experienced only by females and occurs when a girl first notices the differences in male and female anatomy. She then begins longing to have her own penis. This is garbage and has been debunked as such by the American Psychological Association.[18]

Moses and Monotheism was written in 1939, when Freud was on his deathbed. Freud claimed that Moses was actually born into Pharoah's household rather than being born to Jochebed, a young Hebrew woman who was a slave in Egypt. (Exodus 2) In his last book, Freud taught the idea that God was the same as a psychological crutch on which to lean. If so, I say, God, is the only crutch that can love me while I am leaning. My conundrum with this psychiatrist at the Talmadge Hospital is that he was most likely influenced, as were many others, by Freud's teachings. Being a non-believer, Freud referred to himself as a Godless Jew[19]. His most famous book on this issue is The Future of an Illusion written in 1927. Of his many books, four concerned God and religion, though he was a non-believer. *Freud believed religion was an expression of underlying psychological neurosis and distress.* He was to say, "It is still more humiliating to discover how a large number of people living today cannot but see that this religion is not tenable, nevertheless try to defend it piece by piece in a series of pitiful rearguard actions."[20] Yes! Island Boy was and is such a believer in God and His Holy Scriptures. This Doctor of Psychiatry had been deeply marinated during those years in the teachings of Freud. Freud's famous psychoanalysis theories were greatly used before, during, and after the 1960s by professionals. Many believe he wrote the secular bible of understanding the human mind through what he called the ID, EGO and SUPEREGO.[21]

Yes, in my innocence of loving all things God, Larry's accusation, and a psychoanalyst trained in Freudian theories, a perfect storm was created for Island Boy and his cherished beliefs.

Upon leaving, my mother was told that it was a good thing she had gotten me out early that day, your son had been scheduled for shock treatments. "My Dear God, why!" Mom asked? The clerk answered, "That is what happens in this place." Looking back on this time in my life, I testify that God sure was on time for me. This facility was like being held in a dungeon filled with insane tortured souls. This was real life and I experienced it. These poor souls, trapped in these dank grey walls of mortar and mind, had many Friday the 13th horror days. There is a song called, *He's an On Time God* written by Dorothy Peoples and sung also by Lauren Talley. He arrived and calmed the raging storm. **In effect, God rescued me *yet again.***

Chapter Thirteen Endnotes

....

1. https://healthresearchfunding.org/friday-13thphobia

2. www.horizonofreason.com/culture paraskevidekatriaphobia

3. John Ortberg, If You Want to Walk to Walk on Water, You've Got to Get Out of the Boat. (Grand Rapids: Zondervan, 2014) 15-19

4. Genesis 3:1-5

5. II Corinthians 11:13-14

6. Luke 3:21-22

7. Acts 2:1-4

8. Exodus 14:23, Psalms 30, Job 9   .

9. John 14:16

10. John 14:17-18

11. www.augusta.edu

12. Ephesians 2: 2a, 2b

13. wickipedia.org

14. John 10:35b, II Timothy 3:16

15. Matthew 28:20

16. www.britannica.com

17. www.thelancet.com/journals/ articles/...

18. www.goodtherapy.org.

19. Peter Gay, A Godless Jew: Freud, Atheism, and the Making of Psychoanalysis / 1st Edition. (New Haven: Yale University Press, 1989) 12

20. Sigmund Freud. The Future of an Illusion. (London: Hogarth Press: Institute of Psycho-analysis, 1962)

21. https://www.verywellmind.com/the-id-ego-and-superego-2795951

Chapter Fourteen

WHY SHOULD HE LOVE ME SO?

An unexpected event would take place during my first week after arriving in Union Point, GA, while I waited for observation at Eugene Talmage Hospital in Augusta. I mentioned in Chapter 13, that before my hospitalizations, God had other plans for me. These plans would tie into the experience I had on the island concerning Jesus, and Him saying, "Come." *I would learn a new song including these words, Just as I Am, I Come.* I was, as stated, struggling with justification in Christ and in Christ alone. Scripture plainly tells us that the sinner is justified by faith.[1] We have PEACE WITH GOD THROUGH OUR LORD JESUS CHRIST, not because we have been baptized in the Catholic Church, as I had been, but in Christ alone.

My mother would surprise me by telling me that she was now attending church. I asked in equal surprise, "You go to church?" "Yes, Johnny," she answered. "I started when the new pastor of Bethel Baptist came by our house and invited me. I also know him because he is the principal at Union Point Elementary where your brother Robert goes to school." I was elated to know that she was going to church, as I had not known her to attend services for many years. She asked, "Johnny, won't you attend church with me this Sunday?" She added, "I will not be upset if you do not want to attend again." Overjoyed that she was attending church, I obliged her and said, "Yes."

Preparation for my First Holy Communion

While secluded on the island, I had not shared with her that my study of Scripture had brought up serious questions. I had some questions regarding the teachings I had received in catechism class while attending St Anastasia Elementary

School. These questions about my beloved Church were quite alarming and caused a belief and confidence failure that could have derailed me of trust. Satan would have been pleased. As mentioned in Chapter One, he enjoys making one doubt.

God's hand has been upon my life since conception. In fact, Scripture teaches that before we are ever born, God knows us.

You know exactly how I was made, bit by bit, how I was sculpted from nothing into something. Like an open book, you watched me grow from conception to birth; all the stages of my life were spread out before you. The days of my life all prepared before I'd even lived one day.[2]

It was this awareness that even during hard, lonely, and often hurtful times, God knows all and loves us. Yes, I have had moments of doubt and sometimes despair. Nonetheless, I would end my day on my knees at my bedside, telling my God all about it, as Cootie taught me at the young age of three. Paraphrasing King David, *God's knowledge is too wonderful! It goes far beyond what my mind can comprehend.* Even the Apostle Paul wrote about God's wonder. Biblical scholar, John MacArthur, writes of Paul's discussion of justification by faith in chapters 1-11 of Romans. This understanding caused Paul, he says, to burst out in praise about "...the majesty, grandeur, and wisdom of God's plan revealed."[3]

As a teenager, Island Boy was wondering about this justification by faith. Faith in Who, or What was becoming the question. Previously, I had made up my mind, that if God would heal me and allow it, that becoming a Catholic priest was my future calling. Wanting to be a priest was the impetus to my needing an education. I had battled hard against the sharp goads in life trying to drive me, as if I were an ox, into the corral of hopelessness. Now, I was not so sure of the priesthood. I would need to have definitive answers to my now looming questions concerning the incongruity of what my denomination had taught and what is actually in the Bible itself; or worse, not there at all. Although feeling deceived, I reasoned that God would show me how to manage this dilemma, just as He had shown others.

> **The Catholic Church position is: Divine Revelation is passed down to us by either written (Scripture) or oral traditions.[4]**

I had so enjoyed my Catholic faith, but questions were becoming increasingly troublesome, as I matured and studied the Bible for myself. So much of what I learned in Catechism classes was not to be found in Holy Scripture, but in rituals and teachings of the Catholic Church. Any denominational teaching not found in Scripture is not worthy to be printed as co-equal. How beautiful and flesh-satisfying are many of the rituals being taught in the Roman Catholic Church. Many have nothing to do with the salvation of the soul; I reasoned. These rituals are taught as equal with Scripture, so says the Catholic Church. *Traditions do not carry equal weight with Scripture.* Consider John 17:17, "Sanctify them in truth; your Word is truth."

Concerning the dogma of infallibility, it was formally proclaimed at the First Vatican Council held in 7/18/1870.[5] The doctrine of infallibility was again prominently displayed in 1950 with Pope Pius XII in an article recognizing The Assumption of Mary.[6] In Scripture there are only allegorical references to this belief, such as Revelation 12. There are also three other figurative women mentioned in Revelation. They are Jezebel, the scarlet woman, and the wife of the Lamb. The wife of the Lamb refers to the Church and Jesus, with the Church being the bride, and Jesus, the groom.[7] This is a figurative representation of the consummation we have as blood bought believers of Jesus Christ. Christ made himself one with the believer, and the believer is one with Christ.[8]

The Protestant Church position is: Sola Scriptura, (only Scripture). The Bible is the sole source of Divine Revelation.[4]

While the Assumption of Mary, along with other critical issues, is of major concern, there are minor issues where there is room to differ in interpretation, such as the manner of worship. Worship may differ in song selection or order of service, but one cannot usurp Scripture with traditions.

Here are six core principles to be upheld by sincere Christians.

- **Jesus is the Son of God and is equal with God.**

  John1:1, 49; Luke 22:70; Mark 3:11; Philippians 2:5-11

- **Jesus lived a perfect, sinless life.**

  Hebrews 4:15; John 8:29

- **Jesus was crucified to pay the penalty for our sins.**

  Matthew 26:28; I Corinthians 15:2-4

- **Jesus rose from the dead.**

  Luke 24:46; Mark 16:6

- **We are saved by the grace of God; that is, we cannot add to or take away from Christ's finished work on the cross as full payment for our sin.**

  Ephesians 2:8-9

- **Inerrancy of God's Word as He originally spoke it.**

  Psalm 12:6; Psalm 19:7; II Timothy 3:16-17

Beware of anyone who claims infallibility. The Bible declares that we have all fallen short and are awashed in mistakes and sins. These leaders who claim inerrancy are often wrong at many junctures. The Catholic Church romanticizes in declaring the Apostle Peter as their first Pope.

What did Jesus actually say? "Thou art Peter"-*petros,* a small stone- "and upon this *petra*"-great rock or boulder- "I will build my Church." *What did Peter mean when he stated in his own epistle that Jesus was the chief cornerstone, and all other Christians are living stones?* [9] We must look at the Greek translation of which the word Peter means small stone or pebble. Scripture reveals in I Peter 2:7b, Ephesians 2:20, and Psalm 118:22 that Christ Jesus Himself is the Cornerstone in which the Church is built. Nowhere in Scripture did Jesus default to Peter as the main foundation in which the Church is joined together and built upon. A careful study of Peter himself, reveals a flawed man, who even denied Jesus thrice after proclaiming Him as the Christ. God has not granted infallibility to the Pope. He, and we, have to proclaim as Paul, "For by grace you have been saved through faith. And this is not your own doing; it is the gift of God, not a result of works, so that no one can boast."[10] It is the traditional teachings of the Catholic Church itself that proclaims this heresy of the Pope being infallible concerning religious edicts. If they claim Peter as the first Pope, which they do, they must also acknowledge that he was married; his wife accompanied him in his ministry.[11]

The laity should always be welcomed with their questions. Wrestling with the question if the Bible taught infallibility for the Pope, with various other issues had me studying and asking; then asking and studying. If I were to be a knowledgeable Christian, I needed to resolve many challenging teachings of the Roman Catholic dogma not supported by Scripture, God's Authoritative Word. Two of these many challenges are Mary's perpetual virginity and purgatory, which I will briefly address here.

Regarding Mary, we see where Jesus' brothers and sisters are mentioned.[12] His brothers are James, Jose, Judas, and Simon. Jesus' sisters' names are not recorded in Scripture. Yes, Mary *was* a virgin, betrothed to Joseph, who parented other children. After the birth of Jesus, whom she conceived by the Holy Spirit, Mary ceased being a virgin when she knew her husband Joseph. [13]

> **"Whoever believes in Him is not condemned..."**
> John 3:18a

The Roman Catholic Church's teaching of purgatory is one that cannot be located in Scripture. Tony Coffey, in his book, *Once a Catholic*, sums up the issue of purgatory quite well. Little did I realize in the last half of the 1960s that there was a person in Ireland, a devoted Catholic, struggling with the same dogma of the church which I, Island Boy, was struggling. Wish I would have known him then. He writes, "Purgatory does nothing to honor the achievements of Christ's death. It says, in effect, that his death did not achieve a full pardon for our sins, and that his suffering and death must be supplemented by our own suffering in purgatory. This doctrine contradicts the plain teachings of scripture and does not acknowledge the redemptive power of the cross of Christ." He further notes, "I share the view of the great apostle Paul, who says that Jesus '...is able to save completely those who come to God through Him, because He always lives to intercede for them.' Hebrews 7:25 *Since Jesus completely saves us, there is no need for purgatory.* When we understand fully that the sacrifice of Christ achieved the pardon of all our sins, purgatory becomes a redundant doctrine."[14]

I would also add, transubstantiation is a problem. Transubstantiation is, according to the teachings of the Catholic Church, the change of substance or essence by which the bread and wine offered in the sacrifice of the sacrament of the Eucharist during the Mass, becomes in reality, the body and blood of Jesus Christ.[15] In contrast, scripture assures us, *"For Christ also suffered, **once** for sins, the righteous for the unrighteous, that He might bring us to God."* [16] *The sacrificial work of Christ never needs to be repeated again, as was needed in the Old Testament by the priest daily, for some urgent sin, or yearly, on the Day of Atonement for all sins.*

Concerning Purgatory, notice it says in the above verse that He, Christ, brings us to God. Scripture insures the Born-Again Christian of their Heavenly dwelling. "But our citizenship is in Heaven, from which we also eagerly wait for the Savior, the Lord Jesus Christ."[17] Also, Scriptures say, "In Him you also trusted, after you heard the word of truth, the gospel of your salvation; in whom also, having believed, you were sealed with the Holy Spirit of promise, who is the guarantee of our inheritance until the redemption of the purchased possession, to the praise of His Glory.[18]

For the Christian, there are no flight diversions to another airport with a layover in purgatory. Jesus, not any religious leader or teacher, is the pilot. His flight plans are laid out in Scripture. He is the only route to the Father, and He laid His life down willingly for you and me. Jesus was and is the only perfect and infallible teacher who has walked the earth. This made Him the perfect sacrifice to atone for our sins There are no perfect people. "For all have sinned and fall short of the glory of God."[19] This includes Island Boy, the Pope, Mary, the mother of Jesus, Franklin Graham, and the apostle Paul who declared himself the foremost of sinners.[20]

Once a month my grandparents and I would leave the island to shop for groceries. I so enjoyed walking around in the store looking at prices and locating new items. My quest to unravel the mystery between what was scriptural and what was long held traditions caused me to forego my shopping trip. I asked Uncle Bill to let me out at the rectory so that I could ask and learn from the priests. Sadly, after just a few minutes with the priest, I was told that I should not question the doctrines and traditions of the church. Sensing that I was making him uncomfortable, I thanked him for his time. Hoping to have another priest open the door the following month, I again was dropped off instead of going shopping. To my disappointment, the same priest opened the door. "Father," I said, "I just came back to ask you to clarify for me why I can't seem to find in the Bible some of the things I have been taught to believe as a Catholic". I was in for quite a response from him, *"Get the hell away from my door with your questions!"* He slammed the door shut and there I stood on the steps. My heart dropped to my toes. I

walked a few blocks down Orange Ave to what was at that time the A&P store, where I found Cootie and Uncle Bill shopping. My grandparents consoled me and were shocked at the priest's rudeness. Cootie tried to ease my hurt spirit by explaining to me that perhaps because the priest had no children of his own, and was probably busy, a fourteen-year-old child should not interrupt him. I went to bed hurt that night, but not before telling Jesus about the experience. There is a song titled, Tell it to Jesus. Here are its beginning words:

Are you weary, are you heavy hearted?
Tell it to Jesus, He is a friend that's well known.
You've no other such a friend or brother,
tell it to Jesus alone.

Months later, here I was, as mentioned at the beginning of the chapter, in Georgia. My mother was asking me to attend church with her, one I had never attended. I was only familiar with services celebrated as a Catholic. I must admit, my curiosity was piqued. That Sunday morning, the pastor spoke about eternal life and how to receive it. He explained that Thomas had asked in John 14 where Jesus was going. At this point the apostles had been with Jesus for three years and had witnessed many miracles. They had felt His love and had grown from His teachings. Jesus had spoken about his Father's home in quiet times together. Now he tells them, "Little children, yet for a little while I am with you. You will seek me, and just like I said to the Jews, (their religious leaders) so now I also say to you, where I am going you cannot come."[21] Simon Peter speaks up and asks, "Lord, where are you going?" Jesus again tells Peter, "You cannot go where I am going at this time." [22] Sensing the grave concern of the apostles, Jesus says, "Let not your hearts be troubled. Believe in God; believe also in me. In my Father's house are many rooms. If it were not so, would I have told you that I go to prepare a place for you? And if I go to prepare a place for you, I will come again and will take you to myself, that where I am you may be also."[23] Then Thomas says, "Lord, we do not know where you're going. How can we know the way?" Jesus says, "I am the way, and the truth, and the life. No one comes to the Father except through me." Phillip interjects, "Lord, show us the Father, and it is enough for us." Jesus replies, "Have I been with you so long, and you do not know me, Phillip?" [24]By this time, the Holy Spirit had my attention. I wanted to live with the Father in heaven. Had I always recognized Jesus, spent time with Him, but truly never knew Jesus as my Lord and Savior? Did I not know the way? Like Phillip and Thomas, had I been with Jesus and He with me, but not known the way to true Salvation?

I had always been taught that because I had been baptized a Catholic, that I would go to heaven. This, I was to discover, is not true teaching for any denomination. Denominationalism saves no soul. Denominations are charged with teaching Jesus' birth, life, death, and resurrection. They are in unison to celebrate, glorify, praise, and honor the resurrected Christ, who is sitting at the right hand of the Father. Together, worshipping Jesus, our Christ, strengthens us the Church. We are commanded to stir up one another to love and good works, "not neglecting to meet together, as is the habit of some..."[25] Dr. John MacArthur writes, "Collective and corporate worship is a vital part of spiritual life. The warning here is against apostasy in an eschatological (End Times) context."[26] An apostate is also a backslider, and when we stay away from worshipping together, we have a greater chance in falling away from the Lord. He further states that as these end times approach, there is an increased need for us to encourage one another. This augments the need for us to worship together. As believers, we need to be on alert for anything that would inhibit corporate worship. Denominations are for edifying and readying the Church for the return of Jesus. They are for upholding, encouraging, and equipping the soldier of the Lord in all tactics of spiritual warfare. John Piper says this about needing a warfare mindset. "It tells me that there is a war going on in the world between Christ and Satan, truth and falsehood, belief and unbelief. It tells me that there are weapons to be funded and used, but that these weapons are not swords or guns or bombs, but the Gospel and prayer and self-sacrificing love. It tells me that the stakes of this conflict are higher than any other war in history; they are eternal and infinite: Heaven or Hell, eternal joy, or torment." [27] Denominations are to be conduits used by the Holy Spirit who teaches and uses the individual and the Church in unison in making much of God by making disciples of Jesus Christ. They are to serve as an oasis for a world thirsty and dry. They are to teach that Jesus alone is the Oasis who can give Living Water which satisfies the thirsty soul and who is the Bread of Life who alone can feed the hungry spirit within us.[28]

"How then will they call on him in whom they have not believed? And how are they to believe in him of whom they have never heard? And how are they to hear without someone preaching? And how are they to preach unless they are sent? As it is written; "How beautiful are the feet of those who preached the Good News; But they have not all obeyed the gospel."[29] As Christian, we are all commissioned to tell the Good News of our Commander in Chief, Jesus Christ. Notice that traditions are not mentioned. "For Isaiah said, 'Lord, who has believed what he has heard from us?' So, faith comes from hearing, and hearing through the Word of Christ."[30] Notice again that faith does not come from church traditions, but from the words of Christ, through the Holy Spirit, directed by the Father.

> **"We are saved by Faith alone, but the Faith that saves is never alone."**
> Martin Luther

As discussed in Chapter 12, concerning the difference in trust and faith; trust is physical, but faith is a spiritual belief in the Resurrected Jesus. Trust is tangible, learned through experience. Faith is spiritual, given to us by the Holy Spirit. Jesus asked, "Have you believed because you have seen me? Blessed are those who have not seen and yet have believed."[31] Jesus proclaims, "He, the Holy Spirit will glorify me, for He will take what is mine and declare it to you."[32] We are saved in Christ by faith. **We are saved in Christ through faith!** The preacher continued, "For God so loved the world that He gave His only Son, that whoever believes in Him should not perish, but have eternal life."[33] I thought to myself sitting there in church that nowhere did it mention baptism or belonging to a particular denomination. The Bible is clear that salvation is by faith in Jesus Christ alone. Abram "...believed in the Lord and He counted it to him for righteousness."[34] "...but the righteous shall live by his faith."[35]

Preacher Graham then laid out a road map as to how and why we need God's Son. He spoke first of Nicodemus. Jesus' words to him were, "Truly, Truly, I say to you, unless one is born again, he cannot see the Kingdom of God."[36]

ROAD TO HEAVEN
may not be the widest or straightest road,
but follow His direction –
Christ is the Way!

He then read, "For there is no distinction, for all have sinned and fall short of the glory of God, and are justified by His grace as a gift, through the redemption that is in Christ Jesus, whom God put forward as a propitiation (appeasement or satisfaction) by His blood, to be received by faith..."[37]

These steps I later came to know as the Romans Road. "For the wages of sin is death, but the free gift of God is eternal life."[38] How? In Whom? "But God shows his love for us in that while we were still sinners, Christ died for us."[39] Preacher Graham then declared, "Whoever Christ calls, He calls publicly." "If you confess with your mouth that Jesus is Lord and believe in your heart that God raised him from the dead, you will be saved. For with the heart, one believes and is justified, with the mouth one confesses and is saved."[40]

Preacher Graham gave an altar call to accept Jesus as Lord and Savior. He offered a prayer of repentance. I asked Jesus to forgive me and to be my Lord and Savior. I was so excited, through the power of the Holy Spirit, God had drawn me to a brand-new dawn. The clearest verse on God's drawing to salvation is where Jesus declares, "...that no one can come to me unless the Father who sent Me draws him, and I will raise him up at the last day."[41] The Greek word translated "draw" is *Helkuo*, which is "to drag."[42] (Literally or figuratively) Clearly, this drawing is a one-sided affair. God does the drawing to salvation. We who are drawn, have a passive role in the process. We through free will accept or deny this call. How pitiful that many reject Christs' sacrifice on the Cross for their sins. There is no doubt that we can respond to His drawing, but the drawing itself is all on His part. I wanted to be the first one to the front of the church to proclaim Christ. This would begin my lifelong testimony and desire to share what Jesus, my Christ, had done for me. I no longer wanted to become a priest, but desired to go into ministry, telling the Good News of Jesus' love for each of us. I mentioned earlier how I wished to teach everyone to pray. Today I wish to share Jesus and grow and bloom in whatever garden I find myself planted.

> **There is only one Triune God. Confuse His Trilogy with another god, and all will collapse. These gods' ability upon which we could safely build, or stand is ZERO.**

The Who I was to put my trust and newfound faith in, was to be no other than Jesus Christ, the only begotten Son of God. Yes, I was drawn to receive Jesus by the Holy Spirit, who is the third person of the Holy Trinity.[43]

He is one God with three dimensions of real personhood. This triune God is sufficient to create everything and everyone while still being so much more that our finite minds can comprehend. Mathematicians today tell us that the strongest form of any structure is triangular. Triangles come in many shapes. They are equilateral, scalene, isosceles, right angle, obtuse, and acute. God was the first mathematician.

Science tells us concerning human DNA, that if any of its three billion base pairs per cell were just a smidgen off, human life would not exist. Modern astronomy asserts that planets are aligned in perfect distances within the galaxy for Earth to sustain life. Our own sun is the right size and distance from the earth and sustains all of life without potential freezing over or burning up. Astronomers go on to tell of the important role stars play in the formation of the earth.[44] Concerning creation, God created everything including you and me.[45] In Genesis we see that everything God made was good.[46] Colossians reminds us that the Triune God holds everything together.[47] Yes, God is powerful enough to set the stars and planets in place. Additionally, He is loving enough to rescue us by shedding His perfect blood upon the cruel cross. God devised His Master Plan whereby we whom He created were brought back from sin to a life of fellowship with Him, through Christ Jesus.

Eugene Graham, pastor of Bethel Baptist Church in Union Point, GA, to whom I was listening that joyous day, answered many of my questions by preaching and providing answers about questions with which I had been wrestling for the last several years. While I thoroughly enjoyed practicing the teachings of my denomination; the traditions of Catholicism, I Had Been Lost! Now I Was Found! The answers were all in God's Word. "All Scripture is breathed out by God and profitable for teaching, for reproof, for correction, and for training in righteousness that the man of God may be complete, equipped for every good work."[48] How are we to be equipped?

Scripture tells us how.

*"Finally, **be strong** in the Lord and in the strength of His might. **Put on the whole armor of God,** that you may be able to stand against the schemes of the devil. For **we do not wrestle against flesh and blood**, but against the rulers, against the authorities,*  *against the cosmic powers over this present darkness, against the spiritual forces of evil in the heavenly places. Therefore, take up the whole armor of God that you may be able to withstand in the evil day, and having done all, to stand firm. **Stand** therefore, having fastened on the **Belt of Truth,** and having put on the **Breastplate of Righteousness,** and as **Shoes for your Feet,** having put on the readiness given by the gospel of peace. In all circumstances take up the **Shield of Faith** with which you can extinguish all the flaming darts of the evil one and take the **Helmet of Salvation** and the **Sword of the Spirit**, which is the Word of God**, praying at all times in the Spirit** with all prayer and supplication. To this end, **keep alert with all perseverance making supplication for all the saints."*[49]

Without Christ as our Lord and Savior we are defenseless. We are trapped in Satan's sandbox, left defenseless to the wiles of the evil one, and his demonic cohorts. Don't dawdle and be half dressed! The great Greek warrior, Achilles, found in literature, is a prime example of why one should be fully dressed in armor. He was a warrior of warriors until one day in battle, the enemy noticed Achilles had no protection around his heel. He was not wearing the proper fitted shoes which would have protected this strategic support for standing. They attacked in this vulnerable spot, bringing Achilles down off his feet and rendering him unable to defend himself. *If there is one vulnerable place to attack, helping us to fall into sin, Satan will find it. We all need to Check Ourselves Before We Wreck Ourselves!* Are we properly wearing the Armor of God? Today, we use the saying, "Achilles' heel" when referring to someone's vulnerability. A Christian can only be brought down when he or she is not dressed in the full Armor of God.

"Preach the Word; *(not tradition)* be ready in season and out of season; reprove, rebuke, and exhort, with complete patience and teaching."[50] Much as a soldier, the Christian should always be on alert, knowing where his supplies are to fight the battle, and most of all he should know his enemy, the father of all lies, Satan.

Scholar, Dr. John MacArthur states, "The Greek word *reprove* refers to correcting behavior or false doctrine by using a careful biblical argument to help a person understand the error of his or her actions. The Greek word for *rebuke* deals more with correcting the person's motives by convicting the person of his or her sin and leading that person to repentance."[51]

Scripture teaches that we as believers are not to wander off into myths.[52] These myths can be long held beliefs that are folk lore, which are traditional beliefs, practices, legends, and tales of a people, transmitted orally.[53] When traditions, not found in Scripture, are elevated to equal Scripture, and are propagated by church leaders, there is a tendency to shroud the very Jesus they proclaim. Examples of these harmful myths are purgatory, the Assumption of Mary, a history of eating meat on Friday as being sinful, and the Prosperity Gospel which is practiced shamefully by some Protestants. We must not leave out the false teaching that any denomination can be the sole arbiter of scripture. This leads to a particular denomination claiming theirs is the only one which will be represented in heaven. Many long-held traditions are elevated to the same prominence as scripture, and yet are done away with if they become unpopular with society. Even those traditions once considered sinful fall by the wayside if not convenient to the populous. Scripture teaches plainly that God is the same yesterday, today, and forever.[54] He never changes and neither do His principles; those found in His Word. "The word of the Lord remains forever, and His Word is the Good News that was preached to you."[55]

Our sole source is Scripture. "Sanctify them in the truth, your Word is truth."[56] *Sola Scriptura*, only in Scripture do we find the Son of God asking each one of us individually, just as He did Peter, "Who do you say I am?" When one confesses Jesus as Lord and Savior, he or she is professing by mouth just as Peter did when he answered Jesus saying, "You are the Christ, the Son of the living God."[57] Notice the verse prior where Jesus asked all the apostles, "Who do you say the Son of Man is?" Observe, only one of them knew who Jesus really was and is; He is Christ, the very Son of God. Jesus responded to Peter this way, "Flesh and blood has not revealed this to you, Peter, but the Father in heaven."[58] Jesus asks the same question to those who are reading this right now; "Who do you say I am?"

> **"As far as the east is from the west, so far does He remove our transgressions from us."[59]**
>
> **"You will cast all our sins into the depths of the sea."[60]**

The ocean's deepest area is the Mariana Trench in the western part of the Pacific. It is reportedly about seven miles deep.[61] Seven is a number of completeness and perfection, (physical and spiritual) as represented in Scripture. When we are forgiven and washed in the Blood of Christ, we are complete and perfected in Jesus. He presents us to the Father as if we had never sinned.

> **"For By a Single Offering, He Has Perfected for All Time Those Who Are Being Sanctified."[62]**

The word Christ means Messiah. Combining the word Christ and Messiah means the Anointed One. This term is used for prophets, kings and even the people of God, but in Daniel it is referring to God, the Son.[63] Isaiah speaks of the Anointed One.[64] We see where Jesus was reading from the scrolls the precise scripture which stated that He would be the Anointed One. There are many who are anointed for different services, but only Jesus fulfills this passage in Isaiah. To emphasize this, Jesus stopped reading at this point, rolled up the scroll, and sat down.[65]

Island boy went to Georgia to receive help for his epilepsy, **But God**. God had other plans as He so often does! Never in my wildest imagination would I have ever guessed that I would attend a Baptist Church, and especially at the behest of my mother. Mom had never shown interest in attending church. God had moved and worked in her life at a pivotal point in my life. Ravaged by epileptic seizures, trying to make sense of why so much had gone awry in my life was mind numbing. With all the health issues I faced, and then the questions I had about the church teachings, I could have been headed for a spiritual meltdown. Instead, God had heard my sincere daily and nightly prayers. He was to be faithful to me as I had experienced rejection from my denomination, my school system, and by most people in general. I would accept Christ by the drawing of the Holy Spirit as my Lord and Savior. I would learn that there is no condemnation for those who are in Christ Jesus. God would show me, Island Boy, in Jesus there is no rejection.

Upon returning to the island, my grandmother Cootie was to ask me for more detail of what happened in the little church in Union Point. I feel like the explanation I gave her came directly from the Holy Spirit. I asked her if she had ever left a room where the light was dim and then entered another room that was much brighter. She answered and said she had. "Well Cootie," I said, "This is what I did when I asked Jesus to forgive my sins and to be my Lord and Savior. I became a new person. At that moment it was like I had left a room that was dimly lit and entered a room that was much brighter." I went on to explain to Cootie that I would live and serve my new-found Savior and that in His Word He promised to work in me and equip me for further service. Rev. Graham showed me scripture where this is promised by God. Just in the nick of time, God reassured me and gave me faith in Him to weather the nightmare of being accused by Larry and the psychiatrist of being too religious. Remember, this resulted in me being sent to Milledgeville? I had to have faith that He would get me out of there. I certainly prayed that night that Jesus would rescue me "Cootie, He did rescue me just before they were able to harm me." "Yes, Johnny, you have always trusted Jesus." *"Yes, but this time, Cootie, I had faith in Jesus, not just trust.* I had to ask the Holy Spirit, regardless of what happened, to allow the faith that I was now in receipt of to rule the day." No matter what happened, good or bad, faith would carry me through. *In faith I was given peace.* "Cootie, God's Word tells us that faith is the assurance of things hoped for, the conviction of things not seen.[66] This assurance holds true regardless of the circumstances in which we find ourselves." It is better than trust because you are believing in God despite what you can see or feel.

Faith is not swayed by emotions or ones surroundings in a particular moment in time. Faith is knowing God will work everything out. I told her that God tells us in His Word He has a plan for us and a future full of hope. *We are saved for a purpose.* We all need hope; and because of Christ, we can have hope and the assurance He gives through His payment for our sin on the Cross. Cootie listened to me with wide-eyed acceptance at what Jesus had done for me. She said, "I don't understand all you are telling me, but I know you love Jesus, and what He has done for you must be very special." "Oh, it is Cootie." I responded. "I will explain more as we read the Bible together." Many times, the need for salvation in Christ was explained, but she thought she would be turning her back on the Catholic Church. She had been taught that only the Catholic Church held the keys to heaven, and these keys had been passed down by Saint Peter to the Pope. Years later I was to receive a letter from her that said, "Johnny, you no longer need to worry about your old grandmother's salvation. I listened to Billy Graham and was moved to get down on my knees and accept Jesus as my Lord and Savior. I confessed to Him that I am a sinner and need Him to cleanse me and forgive me for the sins I have committed and any that I will ever commit." This letter made tears come to my eyes, "Dear God, thank you for Cootie's salvation!"

In his Bible commentary, Dr. John MacArthur expounds upon faith, "True faith is not based on empirical evidence, but of divine assurance, and is a gift of God."[67] There would be many more times in my life that faith in an omnipotent, omniscient, and omnipresent God would rule the day. Faith given by the Holy Spirit helps us to view God as having unlimited and universal power. We are made aware of His vast knowledge, and finally, we observe His very presence exists, everywhere, at all times. Trust is empirical in that it relies on experiences of the past. Faith looks forward and is assured of the all-encompassing, loving God ruling over all. My child like faith (trust) blossomed by the grace of God, giving me certainty in life now, and more importantly, in life everlasting, purchased for me by the blood of Jesus.

> **Allow No Veil to Exist Over the Gospel.**
> Dietrich Bonhoeffer

Eric Metaxas has written a powerful biography about the life of acclaimed theologian, (Dietrich Bonhoeffer Pastor, Martyr, Prophet, Spy) Christianity Today says, "Metaxas presents Bonhoeffer as a clear-headed, deeply convicted Christian who submitted to no one and nothing except God and His Word." The Wall Street Journal says, "In Bonhoeffer, Mr. Metaxas reminds us that there are forms of religion- respectable, domesticated, timid- that may end up doing the devil's work for him."[68]

In these two reviews, just a few of the many that could be cited, we see a glimpse of Bonhoeffer, that he was completely sold out to God, and that he saw difficulties with organized religion. Christians need to remain alert and vigilant, asking, Does the whole of the Bible support any traditions that are being taught in this denomination? Have man-made traditions somehow been inserted to lead many astray and to cloud the main focus of Scripture, Jesus our Christ?

The labels Catholic or Protestant are unimportant. What is important is Scripture. Some Protestant churches have taken to the practice of deleting songs from their hymnals that reference the blood of Christ and its atonement for sin. Many have also removed speaking about the blood from their pulpits. Without the shed blood of Jesus there is no propitiation for sin. This leaves the antidote for sin erased from their teaching, and thus their congregation dead in sins, separated from Christ, our only refuge and way to the Father in Heaven. Those who neglect preaching about the atoning blood of Christ for sin are impotent. This throws the doors of the church wide open to accepting debauchery from the world. I am thankful for the plain teaching of Ephesians 2.

"But now in Christ Jesus you who once were far off have been brought near by the blood of Christ. For he himself is our peace, who has made us both one and has broken down in his flesh the dividing wall of hostility by abolishing  the law of commandments expressed in ordinances, that he might create in himself one new man in place of the two, so making peace, and might reconcile us both to God in one body through the cross, thereby killing the hostility...Christ Jesus himself being the cornerstone, in whom the whole structure, being joined together, grows into a holy temple in the Lord."

There is a song written by Keith Getty, from Northern Ireland and Stuart Townend from England. Their collaboration in writing this song is an auspicious occurrence, given the fact of the strife between the countries from 1968 through 1998. It is a testimony to what Christ can do in bringing us together. The song, entitled *In Christ Alone*, is beautiful.

In Christ alone my hope is found,
He is my light, my strength, my song;
This Cornerstone, this solid Ground,
Firm through the fiercest drought and storm.

In Christ alone! – who took on flesh,
Fullness of God in helpless babe.
This gift of love and righteousness,
Scorned by the ones He came to save:
Till on that cross as Jesus died,
The wrath of God was satisfied -
For every sin on Him was laid;
Here in the death of Christ I live.

And as He stands in victory
Sin's curse has lost its grip on me,
For I am His and He is mine -
Bought with the precious blood of Christ.

No power of hell, no scheme of man,
Can ever pluck me from His hand:
Till He returns or calls me home,
Here in the power of Christ I'll stand.[69]

Island Boy's life was forever changed because Christ saved his soul. In Jesus we are promised eternal life, and in Him alone. Jesus actually said, "Truly, Truly, I say to you, unless one is born again, he cannot see the Kingdom of God."[70] He said, "Do not marvel that I said to you, you must be born again."[71] When the gospel is preached and the Holy Spirit calls us to accept the free but costly gift of Christ, all that is required is to answer His call and confess our sins. "He is faithful and just to forgive us our sins and to cleanse us from all unrighteousness."[72]

Let us hold fast the confession of our hope without wavering, for He who promised is faithful. And let us consider how to stir up one another to love and good works, not neglecting to meet together, as is the habit of some, but encouraging one another, and all the more as you see the day drawing near. [73]

In conclusion of this chapter, it has not been the aim to discredit any person or denomination. The purpose has been to address salvation of the soul through Jesus Christ alone. No denomination can claim they are the only one who possesses the key to the gates of Heaven. Many do teach myths and elevate traditions over Scripture. Others eliminate key Scripture doctrine and have gone silent on the shedding of the Blood of Jesus from the pulpit and in hymnals. Some have allowed the world's belief system to usurp the teachings found in Scripture. One may ask what to do? The answer is Sola Scriptura. Do not add or take away. Scripture is perfect because God is perfect. Jesus Christ alone unlocks the Gates of Heaven to us by His birth as the Second Adam, although He has existed as part of the Triune God for all of eternity. As His body was crucified on the Roman cross, the suffering and shedding of His unique pure blood was cruel but resulted in overcoming the sins of the world. He took full payment for the sins of those who are given to Him by the Father in Heaven. He came and was born of a virgin, and yet was The Son of God. He alone is able to save the soul through the shedding of His innocent blood which made Him the perfect Lamb of God, who takes away the sins of the world. He died and was buried, but on the Third Day he arose from the grave. His resurrection should cause each of us to ask and proclaim as Scripture does, "O Death, where is thy sting? O, Grave, where is thy victory?"[74]

Jesus alone is able to forgive us of our sins. No one, nothing else, no other can accomplish this herculean, divine act. We cannot be perfect enough, die enough, or burn enough *(if there were a Purgatory)* to remove sin from our souls. There are unfortunately people who are unsaved in every denomination. These people might have gone to the altar to accept Jesus simply because their friends were doing so. Others may have been too young and did not understand but were told by someone to go forward to accept Jesus as Savior. Some were surrounded by well-meaning individuals and were asked to accept Christ by saying the prayer of salvation. There are still others who were taught that by being baptized and belonging to that denomination, they would be saved. If you are one who thinks you have accepted Christ as Lord and Savior, but have not, or care not to follow Jesus, you must examine yourself. A saved person will desire to grow, worship, serve God, study His Word, and align themselves with a body of believers who do the same. They will know that God's Word always trumps man's word. Further, they will have a desire to follow God's commands, instead of those accepted by the world. This is by no means a list of who is saved and who is not. Remember, Scripture says the Holy Spirit draws a man to Christ through the preaching of the gospel. This includes witnessing to others through various methods. Living a Spirit-filled, Christ-like life is the best of all witnessing. "...because of His great love, God, who is rich in mercy, made *me* alive in Christ even when *I was* dead in transgressions. It's by His Grace, I have been saved."[75]

I was later to discover that the imagery I had shared with Cootie about coming into a greater light, was scriptural. "If we say we have fellowship with him while we walk in darkness, we lie and do not practice the truth. But, if we walk in the light, as He is in the light, we have fellowship with one another and the blood of Jesus, cleanses from all sin.[76] If you have never accepted Jesus as your Savior, won't you do it now? Pray sincerely:

Create in me a clean heart, O God.
Give me a loyal spirit within.
I know that I am a sinner,
and that belonging to a denomination,
or the fact that I have been baptized,
cannot save my soul from eternal death.
I believe in Jesus Christ. He alone is able to save.
He died for my sins, and You, O God,
raised your Son to life from the grave.
I confess my sins to you, Jesus,
I trust you for my salvation.
Guide my life, and by the Holy Spirit,
help me to do your will and serve you as Lord.
Amen

WHAT DO I NEED TO DO?

Find a Bible-Believing Church
Attend Faithfully
Be Sincere
Diligently Search the Scriptures
(God's Love Letters to Us)
Pray Daily
Strive to Live a Life Free from Sin
Confess Known Sin to Your GREAT and MERCIFUL Savior
Enjoy Growing in the Lord
Tell Others What Christ Has Done for You
Rejoice in What He Has Done for Others
Edify Others by Serving and Worshipping with Them

Chapter Fourteen Endnotes

1. Romans 5:1
2. The Message Bible. (Colorado Springs: NavPress Publishing Group, 1993, 1994, 1995) 732
3. The MacArthur Study Bible, English Standard Version ESV. Second Edition/Study Notes (Nashville: Thomas Nelson Publishers, 2021) 1565
4. https://www.catholic.com/tract/scripture-and-traditions
5. www.catholicfaithandreason.org/papal-infallibility
6. catholicism.org/America-immaculate-conception-marian-morsels-convert
7. Revelation 21:9
8. John 17:22 Col. 1:27
9. Jashow.org/articles/how-concerning-is-the-roman-catholic-view-that-peter-was-the-first-pope-part-1
10. Ephesians 2:8
11. Mark 1:29-31 I Cor. 9:5
12. Matt. 13:55-56 Mark 6:3
13. Luke 1:27, 34, 35
14. Tony Coffey, Once a Catholic. (Eugene: Harvest House Publishers, 1993)
15. en.wikipedia.org/wiki/Transubstantiation
16. I Peter 3:18
17. The Holy Bible: New King James Version, NKJV Phil.3:20 1711
18. The Holy Bible: New King James Version, NKJV Eph.1: 11-14 1694
19. Romans 3: 23
20. 1st Timothy 1:15
21. John 13:33
22. John13:36

23. John 14:3

24. John 14:5-6, 8-9

25. Hebrews 10:24-25.

26. The MacArthur Study Bible, 1757

27. John Piper. Don't Waste Your Life. (Wheaton: Crossway, 2009)
    111- 112

28. John 6:35, Rev. 7:16a

29. Romans 10:14-17

30. Isaiah 53:1

31. John 20:29

32. John 16:14

33. John 3:16

34. Genesis 15:16

35. Habakkuk 2:4b

36. John 3:3

37. Romans 3:22b-25,

38. Romans 3:23

39. Romans 5:8

40. Romans 10:9-10

41. John 6:44

42. Peggy Overstreet https://greekwordstudies.blogspot.
    com/2007/04/draw.html

43. Matt. 28:19, II Corinthians 13:14

44. physics.stackexchange.com.

45. Psalm 148:1-5

46. Genesis 1:31a

47. Colossians 1:17

48. II Timothy 3:16

49. Ephesians 6:10-18

50. II Timothy 4:2

51. *The MacArthur Study Bible, 1724*

52. *II Timothy 4:4*

53. *American Heritage Dictionary/Second College Edition. (Boston: Houghton Mifflin Company, 1982, 1985, 1991) 520*

54. *Hebrews 13:8*

55. *I Peter 1:25*

56. *John 17:17*

57. *Matthew 16:16*

58. *Matthew 16:17b*

59. *Psalm 103:12*

60. *Micah 7:19b*

61. *https://en.wikipedia.org/wiki/Mariana_Trench*

62. *Hebrews 10:14*

63. *Daniel 9:25-26*

64. *Isaiah 61:1-2a*

65. *Luke 4:16-21*

66. *Hebrews 11:1*

67. *The MacArthur Study Bible, 1758*

68. *Eric Metaxas. Bonhoeffer: Pastor, Martyr, Prophet, Spy. / Praise for Bonhoeffer (Nashville: Thomas Nelson Publishers, 2010)*

69. *www.azlyrics.com*

70. *John 3:3*

71. *John 3:7*

72. *I John 1:9*

73. *Hebrews 10:23-25*

74. *Authorized King James Version/ I Corinthians 15:55 (Grand Rapids: Zondervan, 2000) 1566*

75. *Ephesians 2:8*

76. *I John 1:6-7*

Chapter Fifteen

JOY COMES IN THE MORNING

Psalm 30 is a song of David celebrating the dedication of the temple. What a joyful experience to dedicate a temple of stone and mortar to the Living God. This structure found its purpose in housing the Ark of the Covenant. God commanded that this be built for Him as a dwelling place among His people. God said, "Let them make me a sanctuary, that I may dwell in their midst. Exactly as I show you concerning the pattern of the tabernacle, and of all its furniture, so you shall make it."[1]

God desires to tabernacle (dwell) with us. We were made by Our Creator to serve and please Him. When we do not fulfill this need placed within each of us, an emptiness in our souls prevails. To quell our souls' hunger, mankind has built false gods, and has used everything imaginable to fill the void. Rampant misuse of drugs, alcohol, and chemicals in today's America is an attempt to satisfy the craving of the soul. This longing can only be met by the worship of and fellowship with our Creator. Whatever takes the place of God being FIRST always robs us of our natural longing to worship. Man-made idols become false substitutions and deny the God who created mankind. He demands His rightful place. When false gods rule our lives, the result is the gas-lighting of Satan. He is manipulating one to believe his lies and question the Truth of God. "Did God surely say...?"[2] Sadness reigns when one believes and is fueled by Satan's lies. In contrast, we read in scripture, when people obeyed God and followed His commands, they were full of joy, and desired to serve Him willingly. They rejoiced so much that Moses had to tell the people," Let no man do anything more for the contributions for the sanctuary."[3] When we acknowledge, serve, obey, and work for our Creator God, we are joyful and filled beyond any imagination. This is every spirit filled pastor's desire for his flock.

With the building of the temple, the Ark of God went from being housed in a tent to being housed in one made of stone. As God continued to dwell among His people, He knew the ultimate plan He had in store; that Jesus would come to arrest the penalty of sin. We Have This Chance. Let me say it again. We Have This Chance for our souls to be restored to a right standing with the Father in heaven. This unity was lost in the Garden of Eden when mankind sinned against the God who created them. A Holy God could not have sin reign with Him in His Holy Place. "If a kingdom is divided against itself, that kingdom cannot stand. If a house is divided against itself, that house will not be able to stand."[4] Temporarily, Satan succeeded in dividing our souls from our maker God. Confessing our sins and humbly accepting Jesus' costly yet loving gift, we will one day put on an incorruptible, glorified body, purchased by the shedding of our Christ's Blood. He tempted Adam and Eve with his crafty question, *"Did God actually say...?"* So, Adam and Eve were vanquished from God's Kingdom. To regain the proper relationship with our Creator, God Himself, had to provide the way back through Jesus, who became our Christ. Again, God desires that we choose for ourselves His Lordship in our lives, just like He gave Adam and Eve that choice. Jesus told Nicodemus he must be born again for that right to be given to him. We too, must be born again.

God gives us thirty-nine Old Testament books and twenty-seven New Testament books, comprising 1,189 chapters. With the exception of the first two chapters of Genesis, which deal with life before the Fall, and the last two chapters of Revelation, which deal with the creation of a new world, all point to Jesus as the promised Redeemer, who offers new life.

The true and desired temple of God is revealed.

Charles Stanley writes, "When Christ was crucified, there was no longer any need for the temple. God no longer needed a building; He was free to take up residence in the heart of man. The barrier of sin had been removed, restoring man's relationship with God. To symbolize the change, God tore the veil of the temple from the top to the bottom. The veil was a thick drapery separating the Holy of Holies from the rest of the temple.

The fact that it was ripped from top to bottom signified that God, not man, initiated the change. By referring to believers as temples, Paul was announcing that God had changed His residency for good. He had left the temple in Jerusalem and, through the person of the Holy Spirit, had moved into the hearts of the people."[5]

Upon His death on the cross, Jesus made it possible for me, Island Boy, to become a temple of the Holy Spirit of God. Listen to the great proclamation straight from scripture, "Do you not know that your body is a temple of the Holy Spirit within you, whom you have from God? You are not your own, you were bought with a price. So, glorify God in your body."[6] Where did Christ purchase me, or you? He made that purchase when He offered his sacrificed body on the cross. We accept this salvation by asking His forgiveness. Jesus is the only hope for new birth. He sacrificed his body and shed his blood for me. I will say with the psalmist, in a most personal way, thank you Lord for saving my soul. Here are his words, "Then I called upon the name of the Lord, 'O Lord, I pray, deliver my soul.' I was brought low, He saved me."[7] Though here, the Psalmist is referring to physical death, our Creator is able to also save us from spiritual death, that being separation from Him.

The Psalmist is extremely thankful, as we should be for His sacrificial payment for our sins, especially in light of this promise, "...but God shows His love for us in that while we were still sinners, Christ died for us."[8] When God looks at me, he sees the Holy Spirit within. When I accepted the undeserved forgiveness of Christ through the auspices of the Holy Spirit, that same Spirit of God came to live in Island Boy. I was born again just like Jesus said. "Truly, truly, I say to you, unless one is born again, he cannot see the Kingdom of God."[9] Only Jesus can offer the way back to the Father.

As I returned to the island, the old John did not return with me. I was a new creation in Christ, infused with the Holy Spirit. Not yet perfect in the flesh, but the essence of who I am, living in this tent, was made perfect. My soul had been cleansed by His precious blood. Only Jesus could have accomplished such a miracle for my spirit and soul. The island no longer felt like a place of isolation. Sadness and depression waned and were replaced with hope and surety. I was no longer tempted with thoughts of leaving this world to get relief. These thoughts had been supplanted with purpose in Christ. Having purpose in Christ meant he had a reason for me. What that could be would have to play out. I thought of Helen Keller who became blind, deaf, and mute at three months old, and yet she became a person used by God in the most wonderful ways to help and encourage people around the world. Keller was appointed by General Douglas MacArthur as America's first Goodwill Ambassador.[10]

God's Word truly became *a lamp to my feet and a light to my path.*[11] My future seemed bright and in faith I knew God would show me the way. He could and would help me if only I would believe. I have always found Peter walking on the water a compelling story. As long as he stayed focused on Jesus, he was fine. It is when he focused on the water that fear entered him, and he sank. It was in faith that Peter got out of the boat and walked atop the water. It was the trust and the knowledge about water that caused Peter to doubt. With faith cancelled, doubt seeped in, and Peter went down. If we take our eyes off Jesus and focus on the circumstances, doubt will prevail. Problems we face can be real or imaginary. Doubt can also cloud our thinking when we focus on what should ordinarily happen, a chair should support us when we sit down, but sometimes it doesn't. Peter knew he shouldn't be walking on water, but he was. Peter allowed what he knew of the world and his present surroundings to cause him to be afraid, and in doing so, he lost hope. "For we walk by faith not by sight."[12] What we are physically is not always reality. When we worry our faith, we doubt the ability of God and are overtaken by our surroundings. When our emotions take charge by what we see, our faith in Christ and the impossible fails.

God brings a heightened reality. "For as the heavens are higher than the earth, so are my ways higher than your ways and my thoughts than your thoughts."[13]

When Island Boy's trust matured into faith, I no longer was captive to my surroundings. I was still living on the island. The naysayers were still casting doubt that I could attend college without a high school education. The ignorant still existed and would spew their hurtful remarks concerning seizures and epilepsy. We were still poor, but rich in love.

I especially was wealthy because Jesus had saved me and had given me a new life. The Apostle Paul must have been wealthy in Christ when he said, "I have learned in whatever state I am, to be content."[14] He tells Timothy that contentment has great gain.[15]

Contentment brought peace, and with this, Island Boy could not help but to praise God. The island was becoming a sanctuary as the months turned. Being thankful helped me not to fret. I may not have been able to see my future, but I now knew who held it in His hands.

A Remarkable Happening

By the time I was seventeen, seizures were becoming less and less frequent. I was offered a job by Les Rayen. He had opened a shark fishing business across from the island. He and Uncle Bill had become friends, and in conversations with him, Uncle Bill had secured me a position on his shark vessel. The amazing thing to me was his willingness to take care of me if a seizure occurred. Cootie was glad for me yet concerned that I could be lost in the Atlantic if I were to get sick while on board the vessel. Uncle Bill told her that I was becoming a man and that every man needed to work, and to have adventure in his life, if it was to be fulfilling. He told her that if something were to happen that John would be experiencing a missing part in his life. Cootie agreed.

On the job, I learned to carefully remove shark fins and store them in ice. I would then run my hand and arm down past their teeth to the gut, and gently remove the hooks, thus protecting the hides. At this point, I would separate the hides from the flesh using a sharp knife, avoiding making any cuts or tears to the skin. The flesh would then be cut into sections and iced down to sell at the distributor of fresh shark fillets. The fillets would end up as a delicious item on a dinner table. I learned that the fins were also sold as a delicacy served in high end restaurants. The shark skins would be sent to tanners where the finished products were shoes, belts, wallets, and anything else of which leather could be fashioned. Nothing was wasted; all parts of the shark were sold, even the teeth and jaws. My favorite hide was of the tiger shark. When cured and processed, their hides made beautiful shoes and wallets. I made sure I purchased both items.

Sharks are known for their viciousness and swiftness when pursuing their prey. The shark's nerve center is quite impressive. Even after the sharks themselves are dead, they can still have a burst of nerves that could cause real damage to anyone nearby. I remember one incident that took place on the boat. As we docked for the day, two sharks which I had yet to prepare were laying on the deck. As we moored the vessel to the dock, two men approached and asked if they could come aboard. They curiously looked at the sharks, and one of the men reached down and touched a fin. The shark took a leap in the direction of the men. They both jumped overboard fearing for their lives. Needless to say, upon getting out of the saltwater both men said they had seen enough, and they quickly got into their truck and left. We had a big laugh recalling the fear on their faces.

One of the men thought the shark was lunging for his leg. Due to the fact that a shark can bite down long after taken out of the water caused me to pray that God would protect my arm as it was reaching past the razor-sharp teeth into the shark's paunch.

After kneeling beside my bed, praying, and praising God, I would step out into the night air. What appeared before me seemed to be a cathedral made by God's own hands. I would smell the sweet aroma of the flowers which were blooming all around. Looking up into the heavens, the stars were bright and glowed as candles. The moon adorned its hue and gave off an auspicious lighting to the surroundings. Sometimes I would kneel in the grass and give thanks to the Lord as the water rippled against the shore in the background. I would say to my Lord, "Your handiwork is stunning and beautiful. I praise you Lord, for the works of your hands; my soul glorifies you along with all of your creation."

As a bona fide, born-again new creation in Christ, I learned to bloom where I had been planted. As I did so, more opportunities came my way. As an added bonus, my seizures were far less frequent and severe. I knew God was orchestrating this because the medicine prescribed when I was six years old, Dilantin and Phenobarbital, were still the doctors' choice of treatment for me. I was eighteen years of age, and no new medicines were found proven to work any better than these two. To the astonishment of the neurologists, the electroencephalogram (EEG) indicated seizure activity, but no seizures were being experienced.

After about a year of my being seizure free, my grandfather pulled into a Yamaha motorcycle dealership. To my surprise, he said, "Go pick out a small cycle of your choosing." I was astounded, "Could this be for real?" I chose a Yamaha 90. Uncle Bill told the salesman to bring out the largest helmet he had. "Fathead will need it!" Fathead is what he often called me. The salesman brought out his largest in stock and it would not fit. Uncle Bill laughed and asked if they could order me one from the factory. The clerk assured him he could. Uncle Bill took me to the DMV for my driver's test. He had brought home a driver's manual a few weeks earlier and casually left it on the kitchen counter. I picked it up and read it because that's what I do. Uncle Bill knew me well. I asked him about my being epileptic and his response was, "You talk too much, keep your mouth shut and take the test." I did, missing only two questions. For the past two years, Uncle Bill was employed by Chrysler Outboard, as a boat motor tester. Our financial situation had greatly improved. I could only guess that his surprise to me was his way of making up for the lean years the three of us had experienced.

Tragedy Strikes

These days I was experiencing joy and healing all by the grace of God. Cootie had stayed well, and everything seemed right in the world. Then tragedy struck, as news came that Uncle Bill had been killed. Three Chrysler test pilots brought the stunning news to our door. They explained, two marine patrol officers had killed him. They had turned their boat on his and rammed him. The autopsy report later showed that every organ in his body exploded upon impact. The V shaped bow of the marine patrol boat left its imprint in the fiberglass flooring where his seat was positioned. The officers were not hurt, and the official report deemed this to be an accidental collision.

The funeral for Uncle Bill was filled with sad emotions. He had been taken unexpectedly and in the least likely way. He had grown up spending much time on the Indian River and knew it well. He was also well schooled in boat safety. My mother Mary was a great comfort to her mother. I heard her tell Cootie, "I am going to miss daddy, he was kind and supportive to me and my children. Mother, I know that you are going to miss daddy also. Try to take comfort in knowing you are loved not only by family, but by all these wonderful friends who have come to pay their respect to daddy and you." I looked around and saw the Mayor of Fort Pierce, Dennis Summerlin, the County Sheriff, Lannie Norvell, and longtime family friends such as Robert and Gladys Lloyd. There was a host of people from all walks of life including many of the Chrysler's outboard test crew. Uncle Bill had touched many lives with his talent, and genius. He had been a man of few words with lots of productivity.

Shortly after Uncle Bill's death we began making plans for the next phase of our lives. Things were uncertain as we tried to decide where we would live and just how things would go. One day, Gene, a supervisor over at Chrysler Outboard test base, came to the house and sat down and talked with Cootie awhile. He said, "You know, Bill had an insurance policy, and this will give you a little money to get started again." It was a ray of hope, an answer, somewhat unexpected, since Cootie didn't know Uncle Bill had taken out a life insurance policy through his work. The benefits paid out would allow Cootie to have a house built on Brookline Ave. in the Lakewood Park subdivision.

In the months prior to Uncle Bill's passing, Robert, my younger brother by four years, came for an extended visit. Robert was and is, gifted in all things mechanical. Though I was older, he had so much more experience than me with vehicles. He taught me how to release the clutch slowly while simultaneously turning the throttle for gas to move my cycle forward. He showed me many times how to change gears as the bike gained speed. Synchronizing my hands and feet with the clutch and gears at the precise time took awhile. Robert was surprisingly patient, and it was due to this that I had success with my bike.

While we waited to move, being slowed a bit by the money coming in and the house being built, Robert and I helped my grandmother with anything she needed. We packed boxes and went inland for needed supplies. We handled various things as they came up and the days went by. The fact that I had gone this long without a seizure caused Cootie to relax, and the restrictions about being around water were lifted. Often, I would go across to the shore where my motorcycle was parked and cruise down Old Dixie Highway. The section between the towns of Fort Pierce and Vero Beach, called Indrio, had little traffic so it was a great place to ride. I felt free as a bird as the wind hit my face. It was also good therapy. My mind would think about Uncle Bill and the harsh reality that he was no longer with us. On my rides I would reckon with the dichotomy of being free yet being needed at home. I would not leave my dear Cootie very long. She remained numb from the tragic death of her soulmate.

The Dixie Highway was the brainchild of Carl Fisher of the Lincoln Highway Association. Inspired by an earlier project called the Lincoln Highway, Fisher was involved in the design of that first road across the United States. The Dixie Highway was laid out in December 1914 to connect the Midwest with the South.[16] Some areas in South Florida have renamed portions of the Old Dixie to give honor to Harriet Tubman for her travels on the Underground Railroad during our nation's time of slavery. She was able with the help of many devoted people, both black and white to bring countless slaves to freedom. Freedom is like breathing fresh air after extended exposure to a lack of oxygenated air, which can wreak of all kinds of odors. Island boy, now breathing in fresh air as it was blowing in his face, felt free of the whips of loneliness and the control of epilepsy which had enslaved him. Riding my motorcycle up and down the Dixie/Tubman Highway was symbolic of the vast array of freedoms I was about to enjoy.

We drew close to getting things wrapped up. Robert and I made countless trips by boat from the island to the shore, transporting our belongings. We were going to reside inland after so many years. It wasn't until we put Cootie in the boat and began our final trip to shore that things got quiet. The boat motors were turned off and all was still. Seven of the boat testers formed parallel lines on either side of us as we passed by. The young men stood and saluted Cootie out of respect for her and in memory of the old boat tester, Wilfred Maurine Jaudon.

Chapter Fifteen Footnotes

1. Exodus 25:8-9
2. Genesis 3:1
3. Exodus 36:6-7
4. Mark 3:24-25
5. Charles Stanley. The Wonderful Spirit Filled Life. (Nashville: Oliver Nelson/Thomas Nelson Publishers, 1992) 32
6. I Corinthians 6:19-20
7. Psalm 116: 4, 6b
8. Romans 5:8
9. John 3:3
10. Helen Keller, advocate, and traveler – Perkins School for the Blind
11. Psalm 119:105
12. II Corinthians 5:7
13. Isaiah 55:9
14. Philippians 4:11b
15. I Timothy 6:6
16. www.abandonedfl.com/old-dixie-highway

Chapter Sixteen

ASSUMING ADULTHOOD BEYOND THE ISLAND

Robert, Cootie and I began the difficult, yet rewarding task of setting up the house on Brookline. Cootie would have days of missing Uncle Bill terribly. She often remarked that she missed his grin and his coming home to a supper that she had prepared with his likes and dislikes in mind. He would come in around suppertime and ask, "Shorty, what's on the table tonight?" She said that she would especially like his kiss on the cheek when she told him she had baked him two lemon meringue pies.

In our second year on the island, Uncle Bill had purchased an old Seville gas refrigerator and a used gas stove. He and I hauled LP gas tanks to the island once a month when shopping for groceries. Robert and I would now have to transport these LP tanks. Since Uncle Bill's vehicle was a stick shift, Robert would drive with me watching and learning. The last few months on the island, I noticed that Uncle Bill's death had affected Robert in a serious way. He was to say, "Every man that I learn to love, and trust is always taken from me. My real dad was taken by cancer, alcohol and divorce took my stepdad away, and now they have killed Uncle Bill." I felt deeply sorry for Robert. Though Robert had only stayed with us for a short time, he and Uncle Bill had a special camaraderie. They were both gifted in making and repairing things. Whenever a boat motor had to be repaired, Robert was right there by his side helping him to get the motor running. They also enjoyed sharing jokes between each other. These characteristics have found their way down to the next generation in Robert's two sons, Justin and Robert (Bert). These nephews of mine have natural talent and learned skills.

As we settled into this modest new home, compliments of Uncle Bill's insurance policy, I could not help but recognize how God had provided for us. My grandfather's job at Chrysler Outboard not only brought us out of poverty the last few years, but it also gave my grandmother the means to have this house to call her own. What a difference from island life! Cootie now had running water, an inside bathroom, central heat and air and numerous other luxuries that so many people take for granted. God provided for us in every situation. The idiom, hindsight is 2020 refers to clear vision regarding something in the past. Outside of faith in Christ, there is no clear vision of the past or the future. Jesus says, "I am with you always even to the end of the age."[1] With this promise from Jesus himself, we can envision the future which includes our Christ holding us, guiding us, and preparing us. The end of the age will culminate for us at our death and for some, at the end of the world.

I remember that Cootie and Uncle Bill would discuss death when they would notice the obituaries of those, they had been friends with over the years. They would both say, "Death sure is hitting close to home." This prompted them to buy two grave sites in the Fort Pierce Cemetery. Shortly after getting both of the plots paid for, Uncle Bill's world age would end, and his eternity would begin. I found myself comforting Cootie with how the Holy Spirit had moved upon Uncle Bill's life as he began reading the Bible every morning before going to work at the Chrysler test base. In the last several years of his life perhaps he took comfort in the words of Job, "In his hand is every living soul, and the breath of all mankind."[2] Our conversations would often help her through the day, but the nights were difficult. Cootie would tell me that she could not sleep. "Are you thinking about Uncle Bill?" I would ask. "Yes, honey, I am. Every time I close my eyes, I can envision your Uncle Bill's body floating on the water." I remember back to the days when I couldn't sleep fearing the death of Cootie after her first life threatening heart attack. I recalled those nights distinctly and this gave me empathy for what she was facing every night. "Things just seem worse at night." I said to myself. "What can I possibly do to comfort her?"

We all have natural gifts, and we are to use them. I was often told by my grandmother that I have a comforting voice. Many times, over the years while reading or praying with Cootie, she had fallen asleep. So, there I was moving my bed into her room. Cootie asked," Johnny, what are you doing?" I answered, "You'll find out tonight." That night as she laid in her bed and I in mine, we both prayed. Sometimes after praying with her, I would read scripture to her if she was still awake. Other nights we would pray and then lay there and talk. When her breathing changed, and I could hear her puffing out air, I knew she was asleep. I thought back to when I was three and she had prayed with me before tucking me into bed. Our role reversal reminds me of the book titled, *Love You Forever* by Robert Munsch.

When she was tucked in, sound asleep, I would quietly get up and go to the living room to read the Fort Pierce News Tribune, a daily newspaper delivered to my front yard. What a luxury! One night reading the paper, I noticed an ad. It informed that GED exams would be given in April. It read, Get Your High School Diploma when earning a passing score on the General Equivalency Diploma. I had never heard of the diploma, but I sure was going to check into it the following day. Off to bed I went around 1:00 AM. I lay there with excitement, asking myself, *Was God about to open the door that I had prayed for so many years?* It had now been about three years since I had my last seizure, and I was now riding a Yamaha 350. That bike was quick on takeoff! I was so thankful to God for my improved health and the ability to go places. I told my grandmother what I had read about the GED test, and I was going to get signed up. Upon arrival and going to the correct office to enroll, they informed me that the budget had been cut by the state and that there would be no preparation classes. "However," they said, "We will provide needed materials. and you could use the library to study." I said, "Sign me up. I'm ready to get started."

April came quickly and the test day had arrived. I went early so that I could pray silently in the library and gather my thoughts. I remember praying and asking God to bless my preparation. God knows that I have been preparing for a day like this since I had been denied going to regular school after the 5th grade. Over the years of tweens and teens I had prayed that God would hear my prayer for such a chance. I had not known how He would answer my prayers, but here I was moments before this test which I hadn't even known existed. The test consisted of four subject areas: Math, Language, Science, and Social Studies/Geography aligning with that which high school graduates in the United States or Canadian high schools were required to master in order to graduate with a regular high school diploma. I was to learn later that the GED was created for the military in 1942. It consisted of a battery of tests to measure high school level academic skills. This test is rigorous, seven to eight hours, equal to, or exceeding high school proficiency. Passing the test requires a candidate to demonstrate a level of competency, and to meet or exceed that demonstrated by 60% of graduating high school seniors. This means that 40% of graduating high school seniors wouldn't pass the GED.[3]

I was on my way via the outdoor sidewalk to the testing room when a lady came up beside me. She introduced herself as a retired high school teacher. As we walked, she said to me, "You don't know who I am, but I know about you and how you did not go to school due to epilepsy. I want you to know that if you do not pass the test today that you can come back and take it again." She went on to tell me that students who dropped out of school, even in the 12th grade, often needed to take the test more than once; many never do pass it. She wanted me to know that she had me in her thoughts and that she wished me well. I thanked her for her kindness but told her that I had worked hard for such a moment like this, and that I believed God had heard my prayer. I never saw this person again, but I sure hoped that she came to know the results of the test. I passed the GED test on the first try. **To God Be the Glory!**

Chapter Sixteen Endnotes

1. *Matthew 28:20b*
2. *Job 12:10 (NKJV)*
3. *www.passaged.com/articles/eligibility-for-the-ged-test*

Chapter Seventeen

ISLAND BOY GOES TO COLLEGE

In the book, *The Hiding Place*, Corrie ten Boom tells about her sister Betsie's response when she herself cried out, "The fleas, Betsie, this place is swarming with fleas." She exclaimed, "They're everywhere. How can we live in such a place?" Betsie replied, "God has given us the answer even before we asked as we read in the Bible this morning." Corrie said Betsie asked her to read the pivotal verse again. She told her it was in I Thessalonians 5:16. "Rejoice always, pray constantly, give thanks in all circumstances." "Corrie, that is what we can do in these barracks," said Betsy. Corrie stared at Betsie and then around at the dark, foul aired room. Betsie was even giving thanks for the fleas. Corrie said this was just too much. "Betsie, there is no way even God can make me grateful for a flea." Betsie reiterated, "Give thanks in all things; it doesn't say in pleasant circumstances." Corrie later recalls that she had no idea God was going to use fleas, lice, and bedbugs to keep the

German guards out, so the women could witness, pray, and read the Bible together. Many were comforted and received Jesus during this nightmare of suffering. [1]

The life of the boy on the island was different from that of Corrie ten Boom and her sister Betsie, but in some ways similar. My almost daily infestation was of sandflies and mosquitoes. They were especially savage during nightfall or daybreak. Island Boy learned to ignore them even though at times, being covered, turning my arms and legs black. I suspect that Corrie and her sister learned to do the same with the fleas, lice, and bed bugs. In contrast, I was not having to fear soldiers, my fear was seizures and their severity. How badly would I bite my lips and tongue? Would I wake up if I fell and hit my head or would I drown when a seizure occurred near water? My hiding place was not a house or secret room, it was an island where I felt hidden from society. Island boy had to suffer inhumane actions, but never to the degree as did Corrie, Betsie, and scores of others. Regardless of one's situation in life, we can always be assured that what we're going through is not nearly as bad as what others have had to experience. Inhumanity is most likely the worst hurt one can face. The true value of human friendship is only exceeded by the friendship of Jesus, as Lord and Savior. One of the greatest acts one can have towards humanity is forgiveness. Forgiveness brings with it peace and love, and in return, the one who forgives is released from hurt and unneeded pain. Scripture says, "Forgiving each other, as the Lord has forgiven you, so you also must forgive. And above all these, put on love, which binds everything together in perfect harmony."[2] *Jesus can turn loss into glory*. Whatever God allows us to go through can be used to grow us and to help us. In times of sorrow and hardship, God is faithful and will use the situation for good if we will rely on him and seek His will.

> **"Trust in the Lord with all your heart,**
> **and lean not on your own understanding.**
> **In all your ways acknowledge him and**
> **He will direct your path."[3]**

By acknowledging God and my need for Him, He has granted me a future and a hope. He, not a denomination or its personal instruction, but Christ himself, has given me salvation. My soul is safe and secure in His care. In His mercy, the epilepsy was being kept at bay, even though I was still on the same medication prescribed for me at six years of age.

I was now granted another answer to prayer. It was nothing short of God's mercy and goodness that I was enrolling in college in the fall of 1973. I remember when my grandmother and mother enrolled me. *It was a supranatural day![4]* The sun was shining, giving off its warm rays. The trees and flowers appeared extra green and bright adding to the picturesque surroundings. Cootie and mom seemed to be lighthearted. They were experiencing with me God's providential divine intervention. The unlikely was becoming reality. The college to which God was leading was located in West Palm Beach. Palm Beach Atlantic College was a Christian liberal arts school. I knew if God opened the door for me to attend that I would be in His will. Hopefully, my seizures were a relic of the past. I held now in my hand a General Education Diploma which would allow my entrance. There were still the what ifs?? What if the matriculation fee or any required exams barred me from attending? The one I feared the most was the cost of attending. A. W. Tozer said, *"How completely satisfying to turn from our limitations to a God who has none."*[5]

My concerns about how to pay for an education were soon to be answered. It was explained to me that my job was to be willing to work hard, study diligently, and to volunteer a few hours each week to help someone in the community. I was told there was a man who covered multiple roles here at Palm Beach Atlantic by the name of Colonel Walter Trauger. The kind people in the business and financial aid offices assured me that the Colonel would find a way for me to attend classes. They were correct and I qualified for what was called the Basic Educational Opportunity Grant "BEOG". The Colonel also signed me up for work study where I would serve the college whenever they needed help.

I worked as the bug man for two years. Killing bugs and insects was something I certainly had experience with from my days on the island. The occupants of the dormitory would be notified when their building was scheduled to be treated. That didn't keep us from having some overlapping mishaps. I remember the time I entered a girl's dorm room; I knocked, stepped inside and hollered my usual "Bug Man!" At that moment a girl stepped out of the bathroom wrapped in a towel. She screamed and I ran out the door. We were able to laugh about it later.

My financial package included the Adrian Sample Scholarship. Each year in Saint Lucie County, it was awarded to several individuals who had overcome enormous odds and had contributed to their communities in some substantial way. Adrian Sample was a physician who died young. His family sought to honor him with a scholarship in his name. Two of his brothers were also professionals; one being a county judge and the other a president of a community college. My grandfather always talked highly of the Sample family for showing interest in their community. Before entering college, I had assisted a teacher, Ron Tyson, in helping to start and staff the county's first drug rehabilitation center, Operation Help. I felt God had already put me to work in helping struggling people. I learned much from volunteering and from Mr. Tyson.

After preregistering, the three of us took a walk up Olive Avenue to the dorm where I would be living. Leh-O-Mar was an old three story apartment building. We met the dorm mother, Mrs. Adele Hughes in the lobby. She showed me to my room assignment which I would share with another student. Suddenly she stopped and exclaimed," This young man's face radiates with innocence and peace, look at those eyes!" Looking back to that moment, I've got to believe the Holy Spirit was at work. *Not to me, Oh Lord, but to you, I give praise.* Mr. Hughes was head custodian over maintenance and grounds at the college. The Hughes' became like an extended mother and father to me and had me in their home most every day, right next door to my dorm.

I was taking a huge step into society after years of anticipation. The following excerpt from a benediction prayer by Cornelius "Neal" Plantinga Jr., but not fully attributed to his authorship, says this,

> **"God go before you to lead you,**
> **God go behind you to protect you,**
> **God go beneath you to support you,**
> **God go beside you to befriend you..."[6]**

I knew that I was going to need Him on every side. In reality, all Christians need the Lord each and every day to accomplish His perfect will in their lives. Throughout the coming years, God's grace would prove sufficient.

After returning home, preregistration and finances intact, I had to thank God for the mountains that He was moving from blocking my path. His word has this promise to say, "I say to you, if you have faith like a grain of mustard seed, you will say to this mountain, 'Move from here to there' and it will move, and nothing will be impossible for you."[7] Scripture qualifies this by adding that what we ask for must be according to God's will.[8] One may ask, what is God's will? To answer this in part, "Do not be anxious... but seek first the Kingdom of God and His righteousness and these things will be added to you."[9] "You shall love the Lord your God with all your heart and with all your soul and with all your strength and with all your mind, and your neighbor as yourself."[10] New Testament writers drew from the Old Testament, you might say it was their footnote. In Deuteronomy 6, we find this greatest commandment explained in further detail. When we seek God's righteousness, live and pray His Word, we are seeking His will. When we seek Him, He will be found by us. Ask and seek God's will, and when we knock because we're unsure, God will open the door and show us the way He desires for us to go. "By your word I can see where I am going; it casts a beam of light on my dark path."[11]

In my excitement, I had forgotten about Cootie. "Cootie, what about Cootie?" God had not forgotten me and the wonderful lady who had raised me had not forgotten me either. I thought, How could I be so selfish? It had been less than two years since she lost the one she loved and depended on so much. Cootie had never learned to drive, and my brother Robert was gone most of the time. Who would be here to talk her to sleep every night? Would the walls of this house close in on her and silently shout at her? What if she died alone because no one was here to help her? The questions were many as the day of my leaving approached. Scripture teaches, "Greater love has no one than this, that someone lay down his life for his friends."[12]

Cootie had certainly unselfishly laid down her life for me in countless ways. Where would I be without her? Where would she be if I left her alone in Lakewood Park, out here all by herself? The only right thing to do was to show my concern by reacting in kind. She had always been there for me, now it was my turn not to leave her alone and to put aside my own desires. I announced to Cootie early the next day that I had decided not to attend college. Cootie retorted, "And what, young man, has brought you to this decision?" I replied, "Cootie, you've never left me, and I cannot in good conscience leave you here alone." She replied, "God has not allowed me to live to see you raised just to stop you from pursuing your goals in life. Besides, another woman has not yet taken my place in this here old life!" "But Cootie...!" "Now, no buts, I have told you for years that nothing will happen to me until another woman takes my place. I will treat you like a mother bird teaching her fledglings to leave the nest. If you refuse I will put thorns in your bed; that's what the Mama bird does. I will make your life unpleasant. You need to fly Honey, and I am going to see that you do!" I knew there was no resisting her when she was this dogmatic over an issue. I knew from my raising that she meant what she said. My only response to her decisive state of mind was to defer.

I knew then, and I realize even more today, that her love was a selfless love. Scripture calls this Agape Love. It is the kind of love that denies self for the good of another. Christ illustrated this when He selflessly laid down His life for us. Jesus said, "No one takes it from me, but I lay it down of my own accord."[13] Pure love is the unselfish, loyal, and benevolent concern for the well-being of another.[14] For the past twenty years Cootie had shown her devotion to me, often denying herself. Her only request was for me to be a good, wholesome boy, and now she was sending me forth to become a man of integrity, absent of slothfulness. Cootie was more concerned that I reach my calling in ministry and teaching than she was for herself. The coursework would prove to be challenging. It had been about eight years since I had attended regular classes, with relatively no high school instruction. There is an old saying I heard growing up, "God helps those who help themselves." Somehow I knew this rang true, but the statement was equally flawed at the same time. It was akin to the crossroad decision discussed in Chapter One; the saying puts God second. It says that He will only help you if you help yourself first, much like the worn out bumper sticker slogan, God is My Co-Pilot. God demands first place in our lives and endeavors. Let's not make the mistake of saying, "Look what I did, and God helped."

I knew if I was going to make it through college, and through life in general, God must have His rightful place; First. Praying to my Lord, admitting my weaknesses and temptations, set me on the right path. Scripture promises when we seek God's will, we will find it. "Not as I will, but as you will."[15] In order to help myself, I had to deny myself. Through the Holy Spirit, God gave me the ability to keep studying while everyone else seemed to be having fun. This is not to say that there was not a time where I occasionally joined in with others, but I had to limit those occasions. My pent up desires to hang with guys my own age had to have boundaries. On many Friday evenings, Raj, my assigned, room occupant, asked me if I would join him and the guys for some fun at several places in town. I politely declined realizing my need to master the books unless they master me!

Dr. Thomas Smothers, one of the smartest men I have ever known, would often say just before a test in Old Testament Study,

"Dearhearts, I hope you didn't pray that you would pass my exam today. God has already gifted you with a good mind and He expects you to use it. Discipline and commitment are necessary." We are making God first when we acknowledge what He has already given. Self-discipline is always required by the good hand of God. *Study! Do! Teach!* The exemplary pattern of preparation is found in Ezra 7:10. Ezra's leadership did not come from his strength alone, but most significantly, "...the Good Hand of God was upon him."[16] One way to be blessed of God is to use, not trash, what He has given. It is often our gratefulness that God uses to help us overcome barriers we have in front of us. So, study (In Thankfulness) to show ourselves approved.

Writing in-depth term papers was another area in which I was to find myself lacking. If I was going to succeed, this had to be rectified. I remember sitting in class as graded papers were being returned to all the students.

My many hours of writing was not returned to me. I sat there nervously pondering why, as the professor, Dr. Roger Greene reviewed the papers with the class. I wouldn't dare ask him the whereabouts of my paper. At the end of class, Dr. Greene announced, "Class dismissed, except for you Mr. Woods. Step up to my desk." My heart sank to my toes. What is he going to say? He picked up the paper I had written in one hand, quickly glancing my way and said, "Mr. Woods, I am going to put your paper where it belongs." He took both hands and crumpled it up, throwing it in the trash can. Ouch! He then said, "Mr. Woods, I am going to give you two options. You can take the failing grade I gave you and have this assignment behind you, or you can choose to redo the paper. I will extend to you another week to get it done, but the highest grade that you can receive is a B." "Dr. Greene, Sir, I will relish the chance to redo the paper, and thank you, Sir, for extending this opportunity to me." He looked up from his papers, sporting a pleasant grin. With tilted head, he remarked, "I thought you might appreciate the offer, Mr. Woods." As I left the classroom, I was disappointed and thankful at the same time. I was disappointed that I had spent many hours on the paper and had failed so miserably, and thankful that Dr. Greene extended to me a chance to redeem myself and do better.

Redeem myself, I did. Dr. Greene had explained in further detail to me what he was expecting. I applied his directions and worked hard to research the information he was expecting from me. I rewrote and included much of that information in the report. It turned out to be many pages long and much more in depth. A few days after handing him my paper, he announced, "Class dismissed, except for you, Mr. Woods." I walked up to him with dread such as the Little Train That Could was experiencing when going up a huge hill, pulling a long stream of cargo cars behind it. He again looked up at me with a pleased smile showing the grade of a B on the front cover. He said, "I knew you could." "Thank you, Dr. Greene, for believing I could and for giving me the chance to prove it to myself and to you." I left the room realizing I could compete with the bigger engines, repeating to myself what Dr. Greene had said, "I knew you could." That little student who thought he could, found out that he could. As I reached my dormitory I heard myself saying, "I knew I could. I just knew I could." I have never received anything lower than a 95% on any of my term papers since that time. I didn't realize the pivotal role Dr. Greene would play in my life in the coming years. I have never forgotten this kind man and his influence in requiring my best and in nourishing my academic abilities.

Once again, Dr. Greene extracted my best from me in the New Testament Greek Language Studies class. I had worked all night at 7-11 and had an 8:00 am Greek class for which I was not prepared. I sat waiting for class to begin praying, *Dear God, please don't let him call on me today.* Well as Dr. Smothers had said, "The Lord doesn't accept a prayer when He's already given you the ability to discipline and overcome obstacles." That morning I was the first to be called on to translate from the Greek into English, a few verses from the book of John. I stood up when called upon with my burgundy Greek New Testament in hand. I must have been hoping for a revelation from God. As I stood there waiting for an epiphany, I heard snickers from some of the students. With head buried in the Bible, I thought, *Dear God, why are they doing this?* Double Ouch! I mustered enough nerve to look up and Dr. Greene was playing tic tac toe on the blackboard. He had put an X in the upper left hand corner. He then proceeded to put an O in the bottom left. His next move was to place an X in the middle. He placed an O on the upper right hand side of the board. He then proceeded to place an X in the bottom right corner. He drew a line through the X's from top left to bottom right. He then turned to me and said, "Mr. Woods, if you can play games, so can I. The next time you come to class, come prepared or don't come at all." Triple Ouch! Yes, I did come back to class, but regardless of the excuse, however valid, I found a way to be prepared. I did modestly learn to translate, and that same New Testament Bible occupies a place on my bookshelf today along with other tools of my trade. We serve a great loving God of whom we can never satiate ourselves fully with His words and promises. Who can fathom this all knowing and loving God? Who?

I enjoyed the Greek more than I did Hebrew, but both were instrumental in adding to my understanding. The Hebrew and Greek words may have a slightly different meaning. Nuance can add meaning, color or tone to a word. The old Hebrew language did not include vowels in its pronunciation of words. One needed to use guttural sounds when reading. Later, with the introduction of symbols representing vowel sounds, the pronunciations became easier. Understanding Greek was also helpful in understanding the English language, as many words originate from the Greek language; also, some grammar rules are similar.

Palm Beach Atlantic College had many highly professional instructors who were student oriented, having their absolute best in mind. PBAC was a Christ centered school of higher learning with success, academically and morally, it's primary objective. PBAC remains so today. Replacing *college* with the word *university*, PBAC became PBAU. Its dedication to the Lord remains intact. As in the beginning, Workship, a required program for all students, is dedicated to honoring God while volunteering one's time and talent to help others in need. It has remained a stalwart of the blessed and growing university. It was put into place by Dr. Jess Moody, founder, and the very qualified and dedicated to God co-founders. Workship has been kept in place throughout subsequent leadership right up to today. In his book, *Miracles and Wonders*, Dr. Donald E. Warren captures the early years of PBAC and it's evolving into PBAU.

I remember Dr. Warren speaking in one of our weekly chapels. He quoted Ralph Waldo Emerson, "Do not follow where the path may lead; go instead where there is no path and leave a trail."[17] I also remember Dr. Jess Moody speaking in the Chapel which was once the sanctuary of the old First Baptist Church of West Palm Beach. He told how the church was built during the Great Depression from bricks, many of which were being reused from elsewhere. The laborers were individuals who, in part, worked for God and were paid by receiving daily meals. The carpet in the chapel had been dyed blue with the help of many volunteers; some even students. He explained new carpet was not in the budget and that we would make do with the old carpet that was already there. The school's colors were blue and white just as they are today at the university. Dr. Moody went on to tell how the song *Impossible Dream* had been chosen unofficially as the song that best represented Palm Beach Atlantic. In the first two years of attending school there, we often sang this song in chapel services. In his book, Dr. Warren, a well-respected cardiologist says, "The story of Palm Beach Atlantic University is one of impossible dreams by human standards. Who would dare conceive building a Christian College in South Florida during the turbulent 1960s, with no land, no buildings, no money, and no real support? Yet for the faithful servants given the vision by a Sovereign God: the answer was *We're going to do this because we believe it is pleasing to the Lord.*"[18]

In many ways, the story of Palm Beach Atlantic mirrors my personal story. It has been and continues today to be a life of impossible dreams coming true because of my Lord. There is nothing too hard for Him. I was born during turbulent times in my mother's life. Many setbacks and challenges would defy my existence and future growth and dreams, just as they did in the life of Palm Beach Atlantic. Debilitating epileptic seizures, no high school, and isolation coupled with poverty would present what many would consider a bridge too far. But God! His arm is never too short. Our Lord has a purpose for every life, yours included. In faith, as a teenager, I had a vision that He had purposed for me to become a minister and teach. Who would conceive such a monumental challenge being overcome? Who? Those who believe that desiring to serve the Lord is His will, that's who. God often uses broken things, and broken I was. God uses broken, plowed up ground to bless the wheat farmer with a productive crop. He heals the broken hearted and binds up their wounds. God breaks the proud for the sake of their souls. Yes, and God uses broken down buildings staffed with dedicated faithful leaders, professors, office clerks, and maintenance, all set apart to accomplish what most would consider a pipe dream or fantasy. The founder's number one priority was to honor Christ by equipping young people sent out to America and throughout the world, as emboldened ambassadors of His love. The tentacles of PBAU alumni are felt in almost every line of work, spreading seeds of love, encouragement and each graduate's expertise. The alumni of PBAU continue to show extraordinary skill in execution, performance and technique which is displayed in various vocations, science, government, education, business, pharmacy, and an array of other vital professions.

When I read *Miracles and Wonders*, a chronicle of Palm Beach Atlantic University, I felt much gratitude, directly and indirectly. Most everyone in those early days of struggling; supporters, founders, administrators, faculty, and staff, as well as most students, all prayed and worked cohesively to help make the impossible dream a reality. By God's grace, today there are modern buildings throughout the campus. These modern, multimillion dollar buildings house a state of the art library, modern classrooms, comfortable dormitories, a beautiful Chapel, gymnasium, and a student union to name a few. The desire to start a Christian college and the God fortitude to keep it growing by past and present individuals has nurtured it to a well-respected university today.

The Man with the Twinkle in His Eye

A most notable friend with whom Dr. Warren and I shared a friendship was Mr. Riley Sims. Mr. Sims was a supporter and trustee of PBA. He and I had many visits, and I'm not quite sure why, but he always extended an open door to me. We often had interesting conversation concerning student life at PBA. He valued my thoughts and concerns, and with a twinkle in his eye, he would suggest that he himself would research the concerns I shared with him. It is evident that he did because some changes were made, and even one that altered the direction of the college. Three years following graduation, I called and asked Mr. Sims if he would meet us for dinner. He said he would be glad to meet us. Over dinner, I explained that Janet and I were trying to buy our first house. I told him how we had gotten to closing, where the selling attorney said that there had been a miscalculation over the down payment and that I would need another $2000 for closing to take place. I told him we had given all the thousands that we had saved and were first told would be needed at closing. Under the table, Janet gently touched my foot with hers, as if to say, "Go ahead John, ask him." "Mr. Sims, could we borrow two thousand dollars?" As we finished our meal, I reached to pay the check. He said, "No, this is on me. You and Janet always blessed my life when you were students on campus." He then added, "Concerning the money, come by my office in the morning and I will let you know." The following morning, Janet and I were punctual for our 9:30 am appointment. Mr. Sims' secretary picked up her phone to tell him John Woods was here to see him. Upon her prompting, I walked into his office, and he greeted me with a handshake. "John," he said, "after sleeping on your request, I have decided not to loan you the money, (*my heart felt panic*) but, I have decided to give you the money you have requested for your needs, with just one stipulation. That stipulation is that you and Janet promise to pay it forward over the years as God blesses you." I extended my hand and said, "Mr. Sims, thank you, I promise to do so." "You and Janet go and make PBA proud. I know you will because I have watched you from a distance and I consider both of you dear friends."

Many times, over the years, Janet and I have been able to look at each other and say, "Well Mr. Sims, we have just paid it forward." The man with the twinkle in his eye still lives large in our hearts. Janet and I continue to find ways to pay it forward, by this time many times over, and we plan to continue to do so. Yes, in numerous ways the wonderful people of PBA touched our lives.

Former pastor, Ken Pennell of the Fort Pierce Alliance Church, always believed and taught that if the church or their institutions are to grow and flourish, they must remember, The Main Thing is to Keep the Main Thing the Main Thing! Dr. David W Clark, president of PBAU from 2002 to 2009, says this, "May we, and all the PBA generations to come, read this account, *Miracles and Wonders,* of how God was faithful in bringing the university into existence; and may we be willing to respond with the same level of commitment and obedience whatever the calling and wherever the task, let us say, *We are going to do this because we believe it is well pleasing to the Lord.*"[19] Dr. Clark is wise to adhere to Dr. Warren's founding focus, for too many universities forget from Whom they sprung, and thus, lose their way.

It is well pleasing to the Lord that this now grown man from the island and PBAU continue in prayer to seek guidance from the God of all creation. Corrie ten Boom says this, "The wonderful thing about prayer is that you leave a world of not being able to do something and enter God's realm where everything is possible. He specializes in the impossible. Nothing is too great for His Almighty power; nothing is too small for His love."[20]

While living on the river, often looking southward at night down the Intracoastal Waterway, Island Boy watched the lights that seemed to twinkle in the distance causing him to wonder what people were doing under those lights and beyond. He would often pray and ask God to someday allow him to experience that life. Who knew but God, that just down this same waterway, about seventy miles to the South, were some specially trained and equipped servants of the Lord. They were envisioning a college, that later would become a thriving university. Island Boy would become a part of it, later, even an alumnus? God answered my prayer, and the prayer of the faithful He was using to build PBA. Little did I realize that two births would take place in 1968: the birth of a college and me, a born again new believer. When one is called to salvation in Christ he is called to serve Him. Island Boy wanted to serve the Lord, but how? He was to learn that one's service starts by believing and living for Christ right where they are. Wisdom is trusting God for one's salvation, no one else. He will provide for us and direct our paths for future service.

Dr. Tom Smothers told us in class something that would stay in the forefront of my mind. He said that many people when they are first saved by Christ declare almost simultaneously that they are called to go preach and teach the gospel on the mission fields. He explained that to be successful in missions one had to start in his own home. Then, when this is accomplished, begin to minister to your neighbors, telling them about Jesus, up and down your street, eventually expanding throughout your neighborhood. He emphasized, all along not forgetting to minister to other believers, especially those with whom you worship. If you find yourself doing these things and still desire to do more, then to the mission field of your country or the world God may be calling you. Missions begin close by and then expands as guided by the Holy

Spirit. Scriptures seem to say, Make much of God in little things and I will give you more. Little things are important to God. Consider a large crowd being fed by five barley loaves and two fish. Andrew asks, "But what are they, for so many?"[21]Jesus gave thanks and when they were all finished there were twelve baskets left over. Jesus rejoices in thanksgiving when we are faithful to our families, church and community. His baskets of goodness left over in our lives are to be shared with the world at large. What you share comes guaranteed to be as fresh and nourishing as the first basket.

Serving God at PBA came in various forms. First and foremost, I continued a personal daily prayer life. Next, I disciplined myself to reading God's love letters to me. Imagine having to discipline oneself to read love letters! Having the morale to study and then study again...and again, was another way to serve. Being at a disadvantage when first entering college, I often was left out of the loop by many of my fellow ministerial students. In this, God grew and continued to groom what I might say was a backwards yet hope filled boy. I was an example of not knowing and expressing shyness, even to knocking on the business office door in order to enter. When no one answered, I knocked again. Mrs. Alice Menges opened the door and asked, "Can we help you, young man?" "Yes, ma'am, I came to sign some papers concerning tuition." She said, "Come on into Grand Central Station. Can you believe this young man actually knocked on the door before entering!" I was to learn later that this incident was told to others. They found that moment of me knocking to be endearing, as they often mentioned it over the years. The ladies of the business office were always so kind to help me.

The Stealth Library and the Witty Gentleman

God continued to loop me in, albeit differently than I had expected. Doris Moody, Dr. Moody's wife, sent for me to meet her near the switchboard office. "Dr. Moody and I have been talking about needing someone who could be trusted to keep a secret and to also do a good job of working in his private library. You will need to keep the many books and material from his past and present ministries, in order and dusted as necessary. It is located in the _____ and it has the code name _____. We both think that you would be the perfect fit for this job." I answered, "Yes, ma'am, I would be delighted to help." She explained that a code name was necessary to maintain Dr. Moody's privacy. "Dr. Moody works long hours and finding time away from everyone is vital for sermon preparation. There are a number out of several thousand people who might contact him on any given day. Only me, his secretary in the office, and you will know the place even exists." I enjoyed working there and learned a lot about Dr. Moody's past preaching with the likes of evangelist Billy Graham and other well-known individuals. Some months later, she would also ask me if I would visit her father a couple times per week, and occasionally take him out for a drive. We enjoyed each other a lot and one never knew what story he had to tell that week. From week to week his stories were filled with humor, and we often laughed together.

His favorite place to go was the West Palm Beach Airport. We would go and watch airplanes landing and taking off. We both remarked of their beauty as they ascended and descended. God was to fill my life with enjoyment and many things to do. I often thought about how far he had brought me from the loneliness of the island days. I was so blessed. But God, he had even more in store.

Chapter Seventeen Endnotes

1. *Corrie ten Boom. The Hiding Place. (Minneapolis: Worldwide Publications. 1971) 198-199*

2. *Colossians 3:13b-14*

3. *Proverbs 3:5-6*

4. *Webster's Thesaurus of the English Language. (Ashland, Ohio: Bendon Publishing, 2014) 190*

5. *A. W. Tozer. The Knowledge of the Holy. (New York: Harper One –an imprint of Harper Collins Publishing, 1978) 33*

6. *daily-devotional.org/daily-devotions/before-behind-beneath-beside*

7. *Matthew 17:20b, c*

8. *I John 5:14*

9. *Matthew 6:25-33*

10. *Luke 10:27*

11. *Eugene H. Peterson, The Message Bible: The New Testament, Psalms, and Proverbs in Contemporary Language. (Colorado Springs: NavPress Publishing Group, 1993, 1994, 1995) 875*

12. *John 15:13*

13. *John 10:18a*

14. *Holman Bible Dictionary. (Nashville: Holman Bible Publishers, 1991) 896*

15. *Matthew 26:39*

16. *Ezra 7:9*

17. *Great Quotes on Inspiration (sourcesofinsight.com)*

18. *Donald E. Warren. Miracles and Wonders. (West Palm Beach: Palm Beach Atlantic University, 2020) 11*

19. *Donald E. Warren. Miracles and Wonders. (West Palm Beach: Palm Beach Atlantic University, 2020) 12*

20. *www.facebook.com/corrietenboommuseum/posts/*

21. *John 6:9*

Chapter Eighteen

BOY MEETS GIRL

During my freshman year I had matured and grown immensely, even surviving Guppy Week. This was the initiation week for incoming freshmen. The sailfish is the mascot of the school. Initiation included harmless requests made by bona fide sailfish supporters. Dr. Naymond Keathley requested that I drag a palm frond in front of him as he walked near some of the small water ponds at the Chapel by the Lake. At one point, I misjudged one of his steps. He stepped on the frond as I went to move it and he lost his balance; almost falling into one of the small pools. He looked over his dark rimmed glasses and gave me a stare, and I was experiencing a scare. What if he had fallen in? This guppy would have been the talk of the campus. Eventually all the freshmen morphed from colorful freshwater guppies into saltwater sailfish with magnificent hues.

As I prepared for the sophomore year after summer break, I realized that guppy initiation week held something special.

It was my first time to have fun doing silly, harmless activities with people my own age. That first year I had even taken part in Halloween prank night, where we dropped water filled balloons out of the third story window onto unsuspecting students walking along the sidewalk on Olive Ave. We ended the evening with the help of a guy who shared a room with another student who often went to bed early. On cue, the go ahead signal was given and about a dozen boys went in and took him to the middle of Olive Ave. As the traffic light turned green at Okeechobee and Olive, with car headlights quickly approaching, there he stood in his underwear. Needless to say, someone reported the balloons being dropped and the dorm parents came over and told everyone to go to their rooms and call it a night.

Over the summer Palm Beach Atlantic had purchased a building which had previously been a car dealership. Slowly they began to use a portion of it as the first student union. It was a modest beginning, but the college was attempting to expand a little more, offering students a place to gather. I was now 21 years old. and had been seizure free for several years. With some of her insurance money, Cootie helped me to finance my first car, a 1971 Ford Maverick Grabber. It was a small sporty looking car with a 302 under the hood, giving it eight horses. I called her Shazam. She would really get up and go.

Saying I was excited to get back to PBA for my sophomore year is an understatement. My friend, Pat Lucey, introduced me to coach George Paredes, of the PBA Sailfish basketball team. Pat told the coach I would make a good team manager; keeping all the supplies organized and washing the uniforms after the games. Pat was kind of a big brother to me. He always had a heart for people who needed advice or who struggled in some way. In my freshman year, Pat was aware of my need to fit in with others. Sam Wright was aware as well. Sam was always someone I could go to that first year if I needed direction in my studies, such as redoing my class paper for Dr. Greene. I missed Sam a lot when he and his family moved from West Palm Beach.

God was certainly opening unexpected doors for me. I felt good about Dr. Jess and Mrs. Moody inviting me to take care of his library and to spend time visiting with her dad. Now I was being asked to be part of the basketball team. This was not a glamorous position, but I was part of the team, fulfilling a job that had to be done. I could also study in Dr. Moody's library and study while washing and drying uniforms. Word had gotten out by several professors who said I did meticulous garden and yard work. Doctor Judith Ackhurst, of the science department and several other professors paid me well to do gardening for them. My days were full and happy as God was allowing me to live a dream for which I had prayed. God is an on time God, never too early and never too late. The same could not be said about me in my 20s, trying to fulfill my commitments and making everything fit. But God, He can even use our weak spots and turn them into miracles.

I was running to class one day, *actually running*, trying to beat Dr. Greene before he started New Testament class. I ran into the room. To my surprise I had beaten him to class. I looked around for a seat, there were none to be found. I glanced over towards two girls sitting at a folding table. There was one seat left on the right. Being left handed I wondered if the girl I was sitting next to wrote with her right hand, for I did not want to bump elbows with her as we took notes. Doctor Greene had just entered the room, so I hastily asked the girl sitting there, "Which hand do you write with?" She looked over at me with a bewildered look as if to say, "Are you trying to be funny or rude?" Upon seeing her perplexed eyes, I said, "I mean, uh, I mean, I don't want to bump elbows with you while notetaking. I will move to the end if you need me to." She answered "Neither, I write with my mouth." Being surprised with her answer, I then wondered what to say next. "Could I see?" "Sh...Dr. Greene is starting his lecture." I pondered, who is this girl? Why does she write with a pen in her mouth? Can I see?" I asked. "Sh... you're going to get us in trouble." I thought, it wouldn't be the first time with Dr. Greene. She quickly wrote her name on a piece of paper so I would be quiet. I took that signature with me. I now knew her name and maybe I could find out more about her. What an icebreaker, I thought. Who is this Janet Ruch? What happened to her, and how does she write with a pen in her mouth? How does she write so beautifully? Will she even want to talk to me about anything concerning herself? Maybe she would like a ride in Shazam, my newly acquired car. I really do need to find out more about this girl. Her almost annoyed look at me asking which hand she wrote with coupled with her "Sh, hush up," *Well, I don't hush up easily*, got me back on task quickly taking notes. I would see her in passing, saying, "Hello Janet." After a few times of this I got the nerve to tell her about Shazam, the current *girl* in my life, and asked would she like to take a ride in her. She is really smooth and fast! Looking back on it, describing Shazam in this way to Janet sounds a bit risqué. However, she accepted the offer to ride in my *new to me* car. We stopped and went into Burger King to have a sandwich and a Pepsi. We talked more and eventually I drove her home to her dormitory, Dobbs House.

The next time seeing Janet would be at a Halloween gathering at our modern, or rather trying to be, student center. Janet saw me come in and walked over to speak to me. She said that she enjoyed riding in Shazam and eating at Burger King and would like to do it again soon. We stepped away from the music and others in the student center. We both said that we didn't get in with the Halloween thing too much. I did not mention about the year earlier where we had all gotten in trouble at the dorm with our Halloween pranks. No room or studying tonight, we both left the activities and went walking along the river, talking and enjoying each other's company. Somehow during that stroll, I had become her boyfriend and she had become my girlfriend. A short time later, I asked her if she would drive up to Fort Pierce to meet my grandmother. She said she would be delighted to meet this special lady who means "... so much to you, John." So, the following weekend we were off to see Cootie, about 65 miles to the north. We had to drive from Palm Beach Gardens in 1974 using the Florida

Turnpike if we wanted to get to Fort Pierce because I-95 would not be completed in this small area until the 1980s. Upon arrival, I introduced Janet to Cootie. She welcomed us in and offered us something to drink and eat. We talked and laughed together with Janet telling Cootie about her handicap, called Arthrogryposis, which caused her to have no muscles in her arms and a dislocated hip. Janet also spoke of her mother and brothers and sisters. After sitting just over an hour, Janet asked where the bathroom was. Cootie said, "Honey, just down the hall on the left." When Janet shut the door, Cootie stood up and said, "Johnny, there she is!" "There who is?" I asked. "There is the woman who is going to take my place in your life. I can now die and go home to your grandfather." "Cootie," I said. "This is crazy talk; don't talk like that. I don't know if I will marry her or if she would want to marry me." "I feel a peace now Johnny, I have always told you throughout the years of my heart attacks that I would not die and leave you alone until another woman took my place." I later told Janet about what Cootie had said on our drive home.

Fourteen days later I was home with Cootie when she came from the bedroom, and said, "My blood feels like it is boiling!" In all of her illnesses, I had never heard her say my blood is boiling. I got a hold of my brother Robert, and he came home. He got into the driver seat of my car after helping me get Cootie into the back seat. I sat back there with her, placing her head on my lap. Cootie stayed, eyes shut, not saying a word until we had almost made it to the Indian River Hospital. She opened her eyes for the last time, with head still resting in my lap, and my arms around her shoulder. She looked at me with her big blue eyes and said, "Honey, don't you worry, everything is going to be alright." I had a sense as if she was gazing right into Heaven. Cootie closed her eyes never to speak audibly another word. I say audibly because she still speaks in my heart clearly. Yes, fourteen days after meeting Janet, she was gone; but she will never be forgotten. God had blessed me with Cootie, the woman who taught me how to pray at three years old and had loved me through loneliness, seizures, and depression. I can hear her softly say today as I write, "Come here to your old grandmother, let me hug you, Honey." I find it amazing that I was hugging and holding her as she was dying. I miss her, but never sadly. She was an amazing woman! She loved me and I loved her. I know she is with Jesus. What more could anyone ask!

Chapter Nineteen

GIRL AND BOY GROW IN LOVE

It has been said that we fall in love. This is a lie from Satan, bought into by the public at large. Falling in love sounds so much more romantic than growing in love. Satan set couples up from the beginning by using the fall in love line to plant the seed for the idea that one or both could fall out of love. Here is what God's Word tells us about love.

> **Love is patient, love is kind.**
> **It does not envy, it does not boast,**
> **it is not proud. It does not dishonor others,**
> **it is not self-seeking,**
> **it is not easily angered;**
> **it keeps no record of wrongs.**
> **Love does not delight in evil**
> **but rejoices with the truth.**
> **It always protects, trusts, hopes, perseveres.**
> **Love never fails.**[1]

To fulfill scripture's definition, one must trust and grow together. It is a process, and even after years of marriage, the couple should find themselves still growing in love with each other.

True love comes from God and is protected by Him. Read what love is again. It leaves no room to fall in love or to fall out of love; however, there is plenty of room to grow in love. To grow out of love, one must rebel against the tenants of love, and this too is a process. In the modern era, falling out of love is called divorce. To end up in divorce court means to sin by one or both people when they accept those tenants that love is not. Again, look at the last part of the definition of love. It always protects, trusts, hopes, perseveres. Love never fails. ***If love never fails, as scripture tells, then there is no falling out of love.*** This is rebellion, and God calls rebellion sin. Cootie had always said that God had someone special for me who would love me even more than she could. I would wonder as a boy growing up how such a thing could be possible. Janet's outward appearance was not the special Cootie had been telling me about. No, she was referring to Janet's love for her Lord. Cootie knew that I loved Jesus and that anyone who would be good for me had to also love Jesus. Cootie also gave me a bit of advice should I have to go forward without her. She would tell me after I enrolled in college that if something were to happen to her that she wanted me to stay, *as she referred to it,* "at Jess Moody's college." She'd say, "Do not ever live with family, for much of them are like poison to you, Johnny. They do not serve and love

Jesus in their homes as you do. You know I love them, but combining Jesus' ways and Satan's ways, *it's, it's like trying to mix oil and water.* You have to promise me, Honey," she said.

After listening to Janet a few hours, Cootie knew that God had brought her into my life, and she proclaimed it. Janet and I dated for about two years. At first, we communicated by weekly letters. Satan was working during this time after Cootie had been called to Heaven. I withdrew that January from PBA after Cootie's death. I wanted to remain in our home on Brookline Ave. to remember our time together and to retrieve some belongings and pictures. I had been told to vacate the property and not to touch anything in the house. Since I was raised by Cootie, I was perceived as a threat. My mother threatened to take my car Shazam away from me since the car loan was in Cootie's name and had been paid in full at the time of her death. I went to live with Reverend Jerry Cooner and his wife Polly. They provided me a home and a safe place to live. He was the pastor of Orange Ave. Baptist Church. He allowed me to preach and would ask me to accompany him on visitation every week. We are still friends today and I will forever be grateful to Jerry and Polly. With the spring term beginning at Indian River Community College, I quickly enrolled for one semester.

Over this period of time, Janet and I began corresponding three and four times a week. When possible, I would go and listen to her sing in the college chorale group Destiny, which John Wilkes, a student at PBA, had started. It was fun to surprise her when they were singing in a church somewhere in South Florida. I would walk in, and she would wave at me with her eyebrows. Following these visits, the girls in the dorm would ask her where I had taken her and if I had kissed her yet. When she would tell them "No." about the kiss, they would say things like, "Well, that's a bummer! What is wrong with this guy? Doesn't he know that every girl enjoys a kiss, especially a good night or a goodbye one?" After our first kiss as we strolled through the woods next to my grandmother's house, Janet shared her friends' questions and comments with me. We had a good laugh.

Janet continued to captivate me with her can do personality and with her life that daily exhibited the light of Christ. One such example of this took place after I had returned to the PBA campus. In those early days of the college, the students had their breakfast and lunch served in the fellowship hall of the then, First Baptist Church. As she and I left through the corridor, we encountered some teenage girls in the hallway. As we walked by, several of them began to hold their hands and arms bent to resemble hers. They made noises of "ooo" and "ugh" making fun of Janet's handicap. I turned toward them to tell them a thing or two about themselves, when I felt Janet's arm swinging into my back as she rotated her body. I looked at her and she said to me, "John Woods, you stop it right now! Stop it now! Don't you know that you are supposed to pray for people who mock and make fun of you?" That day, a ninety-eight pound young lady stopped this two-hundred pound guy because she spoke what Jesus said. When I returned to Leh-O-Mar dormitory, I asked the Lord what had just happened. "Lord Jesus, I need her in my life." I whispered to Him.

God was indeed answering my whispered prayer. Some months later we became engaged. We were out one evening and Janet did not seem to be her cheery self. I asked her was everything all right as we meandered down the highway in Shazam. The four guys, Matthew Mark, Luke and John and their friends always sat between us on every date. When Janet didn't readily answer me, I pulled over on a small road that ran between the old Chapel and the bookstore of the college. Janet looked at me and began to cry. "John, I cannot marry you." "What? What have I done?" She cried more and I grabbed a tissue to wipe away her tears. "John," she said, "you have done nothing. Some of the girls back at the dorm are saying that you will get tired of dressing me every morning, and other things." I listened quietly as she recited a list of things they had said, including that John would feel trapped overtime. But God, He would give me the right words... "Janet," I softly replied. "they do not know who I am or any of my background from the island days. They do not realize that in my growing up God prepared me for you, and for that matter, you for me. I have cooked, cleaned house, washed hair, and did laundry. I even learned to shave my grandmother's legs and pluck her chin if you ever need that. I will promise you this, I will never get tired of loving and helping you as long as you continue to be the amazing woman that you are. Janet, you seek my best over yourself, and that is why we are having this discussion. You are showing your love for me by denying yourself. Now that is true love! Let us have joy together and help each other. You always try to do things for yourself, and I have never witnessed you using your handicap as an excuse not to do. You always figure out a way if it is possible. Besides, I love you and need you. God's Word says that love always perseveres, and love never fails. So, Honey, what is there to be concerned about?" She acknowledged the truth in what I was saying, and I took her to her dorm to meet the 9:00 PM college imposed curfew.

Janet and I continued to grow in love! It was the spring of 1976, and the wedding date was set for the summer; July 31st. which was quickly approaching. Janet was leading on all the arrangements. I learned that women get deep into the planning of a wedding and Janet was no exception. The wedding dress had to be one that satisfied her dreams. The color scheme had to be exactly right, and the bridesmaids and maid of honor had to be selected. Of course, they would come from the array of friends she held dear to her heart. Jean Saunders Crowder would be her maid of honor. The bridesmaids would be Linda Warn Rose and Sheryl Whitaker, Janet's niece. Janet asked who I was thinking about having as my best man. "Well," I answered, "my best friends are Pat Lucey and Leslie Payne." I had already asked Ken Long and Steve Miller to be my groomsmen. Ken, (affectionately called Bubba Jack) was my eating buddy back in the day. He was from Vero Beach, near Ft. Pierce, and was always up for a buffet. Steve was an all-around Christian guy who rounded out our circle of friends, much as the French Horn rounds out the overall sound of a musical ensemble. God had truly surrounded me with upstanding individuals. "Pat came by and said he was going to be out of state and told me he was sorry there was no way he could be my best man." Leslie and Pat had been friends, prayer partners and fellow ministerial students. They each graciously committed to stepping back if the other one could serve as my best man. The glorious thing is God is in the details if we give Him place and invite Him into our plans. So, July 31st, Leslie would be standing beside me. I asked my professor, Dr. Roger Greene, to perform the ceremony. He had made a huge difference in my life and education. With great respect, I could think of no other person who I would choose more than him, as Janet and I embarked on this journey of matrimony; two flesh becoming one. Dr. Greene gave us premarital counseling at his residence office. I remember these beautiful words he spoke as he addressed those in attendance at the closing of the ceremony.

Leslie Payne, myself, and Dr. Roger Greene on my wedding day

**"Ladies and gentlemen, I introduce to you
Mr. and Mrs. John Woods, One in Name, One in Aim,
and One in the high calling of Jesus Christ."**

Yes, Janet now had my last name, and I was given a supportive assistant. My prayer to God was, "Help me Lord, to protect this woman who is now, as Adam stated, *bone of my bone and flesh of my flesh.*" "Therefore, a man shall leave his father and mother and hold fast to his wife, and they shall become one flesh." The words *hold fast* carry the sense of a permanent or indissoluble union. One in aim would help us to hold fast to each other. Having good aim takes practice. With every year of marriage, we have been faithful to our Lord in service and prayers. He has taught us how to aim better and straighter. We have been aiming together forty-five years. We are still not perfect in every aim we take together, but the fun in trying gets better and better with every practice. When these words are applied to a Christian marriage, this is how we have success. "Finally, brothers, Rejoice! Aim for restoration, comfort one another, agree with one another, live in peace; and the God of love and peace will be with you."[2] When we do this, we are aiming to please God, what better aim could we take!

Chapter Nineteen Endnotes

1. *The Ryrie Study Bible, New International Version. (Chicago: The Moody Bible Institute, 1986) 1582-1583*
2. *II Corinthians 13:11*

Chapter Twenty

THE JOURNEY CONTINUES

Janet journeyed from South Bend, Indiana to attend PBA. I journeyed from Fort Pierce Florida. The city's name, South Bend, hails from the southernmost bend of the Saint Joseph River where the city first began.[1] The name Fort Pierce originates from Officer Benjamin Pierce, commander of the early local cavalry garrison. Benjamin was the brother of Franklin Pierce, the 14th president of the United States.[2] We both were continuing our journeys to which God had called us, but now there were two of us sharing and merging upon each other's path. God uses, even today, this sometimes rocky and steep path we travel to build character and to keep our reliance on Him. The last two years at PBA were financially tough, but the flame of our dreams and the assurance of God's calling upon each of us never decreased. It was much like the flame of the burning bush that Moses encountered in Exodus 3:2. The flames kept burning and the bush was never consumed, neither was the voice calling to him diminished. Our textbooks were purchased even if there wasn't any money left over for food that month for dinners or on weekends when the school's cafeteria was closed.

When Janet was 18, she had been declared 100% disabled. Her body might have been given this title, but not her spirit, always reaching for that unreachable star. She believed as I did, in reaching for that star of service, which many said would be impossible. It is always possible when God is being worshipped. Scripture teaches, "**Surely the arm of the LORD is not too short to save.**"[3] Our great, wonderful God sees our future and maps it out even when we are yet to be. "Like an open book, you watched me grow from conception to birth; all the stages of my life were spread out before you. The days of my life all prepared before I'd even lived one day."[4] Our God knew the desires He had placed in my heart, and in Janet's heart; so too He knows the desires of those reading this book. **One needs to be careful here in what is being said.** *In Psalm 37:4 we read, "Delight yourself in the Lord, and He will give you the desires of your heart." God gives us the desires of our hearts but note! He does not give us our heart's desire. We must first do what? Delight ourselves in the Lord.* Delighting in the Lord entails things like, loving one another, obeying the Lord, being kind and forgiving. It involves justice and mercy and serving one another, as well as maintaining a prayer life, worshipping and regularly reading His Word, He has so graciously provided for us. This is just to name a few. **When we delight ourselves in God, what we desire will be what He desires.** As mentioned, Janet was told that she was declared to be unable to work. As a result, she received Supplemental Security Income. (SSI) Due to our financial needs, this would have helped us a lot, but this was not to be. The Social Security office stipulated that if Janet were to marry, she would not be head of household, thus her disability benefits would be stopped. They would have allowed her to continue benefits if we had just lived together and not obeyed God in holy matrimony. Yes, money was needed, but delighting our God through obedience to His will was much more important. We knew deep in our hearts that *God responds to righteousness; not ours, but His*. We are righteous only in His righteousness. We both knew that if we delighted in God He would surely make a way. God will provide a way for anyone who delights in Him. The way may seem steep but the alternative way, outside of God's will, always turns out to be steeper and more treacherous. Here is what God says about it, "You will find rest for your souls. For my yoke is easy and my burden is light."[5]

Janet and I were blessed by choosing right and we experienced the joy of this, "Therefore, I tell you, do not be anxious about your life, what you will eat or what you will drink, nor about your body, what you will put on. Is not life more than food, and the body more than clothing? Look at the birds of the air. Consider the lilies of the field, how they grow: they neither toil or spin, but seek first the Kingdom of God and His righteousness and all these things will be added to you."[6]

Graduation day at Palm Beach Atlantic arrived for Janet and me. She received the Outstanding Senior Woman award. I finished knowing that with every year of college, success had come to a very thankful young man.

The week before graduation, I would hear a car beep at me as it was passing by on Olive Ave. I realized that it was one of the ministerial students. He finished his degree before Christmas. He pulled over into the parking lot across from Leh-O-Mar dorm. He asked me if he could buy me a steak dinner. "Yes," I replied, "but what for?" "Get in and I will explain on our way to the steakhouse." He told me that he had come to PBA looking for me explicitly. His reason really touched my heart. He explained, "John, during the first few months starting our ministerial degree preparation, a group of us guys got together and discussed among ourselves who would make it to graduation, who would finish and who wouldn't. We chose you to be the least likely to make it through to graduation. We often did not include you among ourselves, but you proved us wrong. In fact," he said, "some of those same people did not make it. I want to tell you how sorry I am and to tell you congratulations!" As we finished our conversation while eating a rib eye, I told him how appreciative I was, and that he represented the best of what ministers should be; humble, gracious, caring, educated in how to teach and share the gospel of Jesus Christ. You have shared Jesus with me this day by living for Him. I will never forget his touch on my life that day. To say I was blessed, yes, I was, but his touch on my life that moment in time is an award that I will always hang on the wall of my heart.

The following day, I saw my friend Pat Lucey on campus. I had just paid for Janet's graduation gown and was glad to tell him the good news. He asked if I had gotten my gown. I told him no, that for now I was excited about being able to afford Janet's gown. I went on my merry way. I knew that if I could not afford to buy mine, something would work out. That evening Pat brought me my graduation gown. "How did you get this?" I asked. "I went to Colonel Traugher's office and told him you didn't have your gown yet. He gave me the money. He told me to go get it and let you know that you did not need to worry about paying him back." We had previously been fitted for our gowns and now we were set to walk and graduate on April 28th. This would be my first graduation ever. My mind raced back to when I was told that I could not return to school after the 5th grade. I thought, "Dear God, look what you have done. To make it even better, you have given me the wife that Cootie said you would provide for me." Only by God's mercy and grace would I still be seizure free, earn my GED, go to a Christian four year liberal arts college, get married to the perfect helpmeet and graduate with her; all this in a five year span. Do not tell me that God does not hear, see, and act if we seek to glorify and delight in Him.

The baccalaureate dinner was held the day before graduation. This dinner was set aside to honor the graduates along with their families. The president of PBA, Dr. George Borders, would be our keynote speaker. He would welcome the families and then say a few words about the graduates being represented at each table. With our names ending in W, we were to first hear a lot of true stories about our fellow graduates and their ups and downs reaching this moment. When President Borders addressed Janet and me, he told a fictional, yet based in fact story. He said, "The other day I passed Janet and John sitting at the tables just outside the administration building. As I passed by, I overheard them talking about their finances. John said to Janet that they had just received a notice from their bank that they were overdrawn. Janet replied with, 'How can this be, we still have checks?'" Those assembled at this propitious occasion broke out in laughter. "No," he said, "We at PBA have come to know and love John and Janet. They have overcome extreme hardships and physical disabilities both seen and unseen." Everyone applauded.

The next morning before graduation practice began, Janet noticed that there were four steps leading to the stage. "John, I can't walk up those steps," she exclaimed! I told her I had come in earlier and that I noticed the steps also and had figured out a way for her to get on stage. "We will do the same thing that we do when going up in the stands as we watch the PBA Sailfish play basketball." She said, "John, this will work, because alphabetically my name comes before yours. I am JA and you are JO, and besides, we've had lots of practice going up at the games!" "Exactly, where there's a will, God will provide the way." That understanding has become a go to line throughout our many wonderful years of marriage.

At commencement, the keynote speaker asked this question, "Under normal circumstances, what line of work would college students miss the most if that work was not being done?" His answer was, "It would be those jobs known as dirty jobs." His point was to never think you, or your line of work is better or more important just because you hold a job that requires a college degree. He asked, "What would happen if your garbage was not picked up in your neighborhood? What would happen if a sewer line broke and there was no one to fix it? What if... The person most people would miss first probably would not be one that held a degree." He said, "Don't get me wrong, your job will be important also, but who will be missed first?" I have never forgotten that speech. It certainly does help to make us realize how important everyone is, and the job they perform to keep society going.

The moment we were waiting for had finally arrived. The graduates were assembled in rows. When our row was called, we filed toward the left side of the stage. With anticipation we waited. Dr. George Borders looked our way and Janet's name was read, *Janet Ruch Woods*. Janet stood sideways as I pushed and steadied her up each step. I stepped back down and watched my dear wife as she walked across the stage. Dr. Borders congratulated Janet and gently slipped her diploma under her arm. She walked ahead to the right side of the stage and waited. Dr. Borders then looked my way, and I heard my name, *John Michael Woods*. I walked over to him where he handed me my diploma with a good strong handshake. "Congratulations, John!" I walked over where Janet waited, slipped my arm under hers and we proceeded carefully to descend the stage. As she and I came down together, our graduating class stood up and began to clap and cheer for us. After they stood and clapped, all the parents, relatives, and friends stood up and applauded us. I remember looking back on the stage at Dr. Borders. He was smiling and applauding. His gentle smile of approval and joy for us at that moment was to live in my memory. As things quieted down and the last diploma was awarded, Dr. Borders looked toward the class and gave the final charge, "Move your tassels!" He then pronounced, "Ladies and gentlemen, I present to you the class of 1978!" Everyone again stood and applauded with cheers for the graduating class. It was a momentous day for all of us and one of surreal emotion for me, the former Island Boy who once wondered what lay beyond those lights that appeared so enchanting down the river. As he pictured himself as a teenager sitting on the southwest bank of the island, little did he realize that beyond those twinkling lights he would one day live. Only an all loving Omnipotent God would know that he would be a married man and a graduate from a Christian college. Interestingly, the college was founded and built close to the same Intracoastal Waterway where Island Boy grew up with his many dreams and prayers. Yes, only an Omnipresent God, who's power and knowledge extend to all parts of His creation, would see Johnny, living much like Gilligan and the crew lived, waiting to be rescued.

Chapter Twenty Endnotes

1. https://en.wikipedia.org/wiki/South_Bend,_Indiana
2. https://en.wikipedia.org/wiki/Franklin_Pierce
3. Isaiah 59:1a
4. Psalm 139:16
5. Matthew 11:29b-30

Chapter Twenty-One

WE'VE ONLY JUST BEGUN

Following graduation, the Lord continued to guide us on our journey. We saw Him protecting us from some of Satan's traps which he cunningly sets for our demise. We were to learn in life that often Satan will try to attack just before something good is about to happen, or just after God has shown His special kindness and goodness. Satan sows bewilderment. We overcame bewildering events by seeking God through prayer, scripture and sometimes fasting. The Christian must seek God's will by seeking His face in times of doubt or confusion. "I sought the Lord and He answered me and delivered me from all my fears."[1]

The birth of our son, Joshua, blessed our lives just fifteen months after we graduated from PBA. Born in Fort Worth, Joshua was an armful of pure joy. As I held him that first time, little did I realize by the age of five, not only would Joshua be playing T-Ball, but would become the Atlanta Braves' very best fan, and has remained so for the last thirty-seven years. After leaving Turner Field one evening, when

Josh was about twelve, he stopped me, looked up at the skyline of downtown Atlanta and proclaimed, "Daddy, look at this view! Someday I'm going to live here! I might even work for the Braves!" He is a son that every father would desire to have at his side. Having had such a restricted teen life myself, God was to bless me immensely through my son, and now, through his family. They love the Lord, and that is the biggest blessing of all.

In the early days, I had become the associate pastor at Oakwood Terrace Baptist Church in Euless, Texas, under Pastor Ludwig Otto. He affectionately referred to me as a *diamond in the rough waiting to be discovered.* At Oakwood Terrace, I, along with my willing and capable wife at my side, labored to have influence in their lives. Many have remained friends over the years though the miles separate us. With fondness, I remember a particular man who would not attend church with his wife. He refused to let any pastor visit him. I made his acquaintance at the invite of his wife, and he must have taken a liking to us, because he asked us to come back and visit again. We told him if he did not feel comfortable coming to church that we would come during the Sunday school hour and have Christian fellowship and Bible reading with him. He seemed OK with that and our many times together during the Sunday school hour turned out to be fruitful and beneficial to our friend and to the rest of his family. Janet and I also worked part time for evangelist James Robison. It was here that I received many opportunities to use my counseling skills learned from my wonderful professor and PBA founder, Dr. Jess Moody.

Between employment, attending seminary, and being new parents, Janet and I were stretched to a crisis point in our health. Normally I would be getting about four hours of sleep at night, and Janet was often left alone with our newborn son. It was at this point that we decided to put everything we owned in storage with every intention of returning to Texas. We resigned our duties of service, temporarily, knowing we would be back. But God! God often had other plans. We spent some time with Janet's sister and her husband, Anita and Herb. We then made it back to Florida, where my sister, you guessed it, Rose Marie helped us to get settled while we waited on the Lord about what we were to do.

Needing to make some money, I went to work as a substitute teacher. While subbing at Dan McCarty Middle School, the assistant principal approached me one day and said, "Mr. Woods, if you get your certification and pass the Florida Teachers Exam, we would like to hire you." At this point I wondered what God was doing. I was aware that a new teacher had to search diligently to get a job, and I was not even looking for a teaching job because I had every intention of returning to Fort Worth. I wanted to finish my seminary degree. I sought the Lord in prayer about the three of us returning to Fort Worth. My mind continued to replay what the assistant principal had said to me on different occasions. "John, you are talented and have a unique way in getting students to learn and succeed." Coupled with the advice and encouragement I had received in Texas for my dealings with youth there,

I wondered what God was saying. I had always thought I would be the pastor of a church. Bewildered? No, because I had been seeking God's will in my life, and if this was His will, then I wanted to follow it completely.

I began looking into certification with the state of Florida and checking my transcript for appropriate foundational courses that I would need. I learned I already had enough coursework from PBA to certify me in two areas. I took the subject area exams and passed them. I then proceeded to take the Florida Teachers Exam which was a 6 hour event. I surmised that God was getting me ready to teach because I passed it as well. The test covered math, language science, geography, history, and an array of other subjects. I surely was thankful for my professors at PBA, as they had prepared me in such a wonderful way.

I found my pulpit in the public school classroom. It was somewhat like being on the mission field. I knew that my expertise was helping students succeed morally and academically; those students who had been in trouble or just did not like being in school. To help rescue these students, I had to find a way to share Jesus with them. I poured my life into them, even going to their homes to wake them up in the morning if they were wanting to sleep in. We do not change people. The change in anyone comes directly from God.

One day, soon after I went to work, I was sitting at my desk, and I asked God why he had changed my direction of service. Almost immediately it occurred to me, *or He told me*, "This is the same school that you would have attended as a middle school student if you had been allowed to attend. You weren't allowed, remember John, you had to quit because of your seizures." I remembered it all too well. No, I didn't get to attend, middle or high school, but He had, by His design and Grace, allowed me this moment. To walk into the classroom as a certified teacher and to help those students who were having a rough time educationally and personally was my honor and privilege. This former Island Boy was blessed by God with opportunities to serve the Great I Am!

Doctor Donald Warren, trustee of Palm Beach Atlantic University, from his book, *Miracles and Wonders*, reminds us of this, "I think no matter what our station in life might be, our job is to pray and ask God to show us what He wants us to do, and then do it, no matter how difficult. Yes, the work may prove astonishing, but through Him we will do valiantly, He promises it in His Word."[2]

Final thoughts: I'd like to pass this on to all. No one is an island unto himself. We are not self-made but are a composite of our many interactions with a Just and Loving God. He then brings people into our lives to help us succeed and soar to heights unknown. We rarely know beforehand what Divine Appointments are before us, but we should consider every interruption and interaction we have with another person as having the potential to be an appointment from God.

"I thank my God upon every remembrance of you."[3]

"His divine power has granted to us all things that pertain to life and godliness, through the knowledge of Him who called us to His own glory and excellence."[4]

Delight yourself in Him, prepare, and make ready to serve.

Chapter Twenty One Endnotes

1. *Psalm 34:4*
2. *Donald E. Warren. Miracles and Wonders. (West Palm Beach: Palm Beach Atlantic University, 2020) 66*
3. *Philippians 1:3a*
4. *II Peter 1:3*

BIBLIOGRAPHY

American Heritage Dictionary/Second College Edition. (Boston: Houghton Mifflin Company, 1982, 1985, 1991)

Authorized King James Version. (Grand Rapids: Zondervan, 2000) All scripture cited as KJV is quoted from this source. All rights reserved.

Coffey, Tony. Once a Catholic. (Eugene: Harvest House Publishers, 1993)

Gay, Peter. A Godless Jew: Freud, Atheism, and the Making of Psychoanalysis Edition 1. (New Haven: Yale University Press, 1989)

Gurian, Michael. The Wonder of Boys. (New York: Jeremy P. Tarcher/Penguin/Penguin Group USA Inc., 1996, 2006)

Holman Bible Dictionary. (Nashville: Holman Bible Publishers, 1991)

The Holy Bible, New King James Version NKJV. (Nashville:

Thomas Nelson Publishers, 1983, 1985, 1990) All scripture cited as NKJV is quoted from this source. All rights reserved.

The MacArthur Study Bible, English Standard Version ESV. (Nashville: Thomas Nelson Publishers, 2021) All scripture, unless otherwise noted, is quoted from this source. All rights reserved.

Metaxas, Eric. Bonhoeffer: Pastor, Martyr, Prophet, Spy. (Nashville: Thomas Nelson Publishers, 2010)

Moody, Jess. Club Sandwich Goes Great With Chicken Soup. (Nashville: Broadman & Holman Publishers,1999)

Ortberg, John. If You Want to Walk on Water, You've Got to Get Out of the Boat. (Grand Rapids: Zondervan, 2014)

Peterson, Eugene H. The Message Bible: The New Testament, Psalms, and Proverbs in Contemporary Language. (Colorado Springs: NavPress Publishing Group, 1993, 1994, 1995)

Piper, John. Don't Waste Your Life. (Wheaton: Crossway, 2009)

Ryrie Study Bible New International Version. (Chicago: The Moody Bible Institute, 1986)

Stanley, Charles. The Wonderful Spirit Filled Life. (Nashville: Oliver Nelson/Thomas Nelson Publishers, 1992)

Ten Boom, Corrie with John and Elizabeth Sherrill. The Hiding Place. (Minneapolis: Worldwide Publications, 1971)

Tozer, A. W. The Knowledge of the Holy. (New York: Harper One – an Imprint of Harper Collins Publishing, 1978)

Warren, Donald E. Miracles and Wonders. (West Palm Beach: Palm Beach Atlantic University, 2020)

Webster's Thesaurus of the English Language. (Ashland, Ohio: Bendon Publishing, 2014)

Made in the USA
Columbia, SC
20 April 2022